AF380900

Van Gogh
A Life in Places

Juliet Heslewood

Published in 2019 by

Unicorn, an imprint of Unicorn Publishing Group LLP

5 Newburgh Street

London

W1F 7RG

www.unicornpublishing.org

ISBN 978-1-911604-64-8

10 9 8 7 6 5 4 3 2 1

Designed by Matt Carr

Printed in India by Imprint Press Ltd

Van Gogh
A Life in Places

Juliet Heslewood

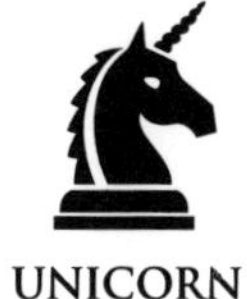

UNICORN

"FOR ME IT'S A MATTER OF LEARNING TO
DRAW WELL, TO BE MASTER EITHER OF MY
PENCIL OR MY CHARCOAL OR MY BRUSH;
ONCE THAT'S ACHIEVED I'LL DO GOOD
THINGS ALMOST NO MATTER WHERE..."

Vincent van Gogh, September, 1880

INTRODUCTION

Vincent van Gogh (1853–90) spent all his troubled, shortened life in four of the westernmost countries of Europe. From his native Netherlands, he set out on a geographical circle that led to nearby Belgium, England and France in pursuit of diverse professional activities. Due to his unsound mental health, failure was a repeated disappointment to him and his family, but once he found art to be his mission, he persevered on this single path.

Wherever Vincent stayed he took pleasure in walking. This was not a gentle amble, but at an energetic pace when he covered several kilometres an hour. He studied nature with a keen eye and recorded its changing nuances and colours in words, drawings and paintings. Much is known about Vincent's life, thanks to his compulsive letter writing. When he lived apart from his younger brother, Theo (1857–91), he wrote tirelessly to him describing his daily life, the artists he admired, the books he read, his hopes and his fears. Without Theo's financial support Vincent would not have been able to pursue his career as an artist.

The art world was familiar to the Van Gogh family. Vincent's uncle was a partner of an internationally successful company, Goupil & Cie, dealers in print reproductions of fine art. While Theo worked for their Paris branch, Vincent's most significant move was to join his brother in the French capital, which was then the centre of European artistic activity.

Vincent's personal fulfilment was to draw and to paint, work he described as a 'lightning conductor' for his longstanding illness. From the bleak heathland of the north to the sun-filled plains of Provence and the rising plateau at Auvers, he worked in isolation, unaware that his achievement would one day be considered the work of a genius.

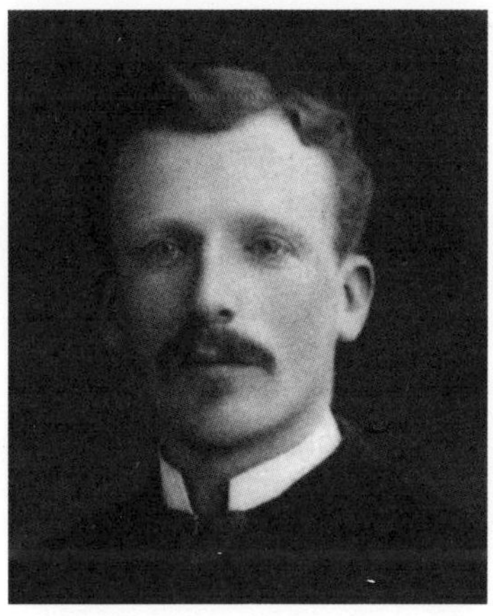

Theo van Gogh in 1887

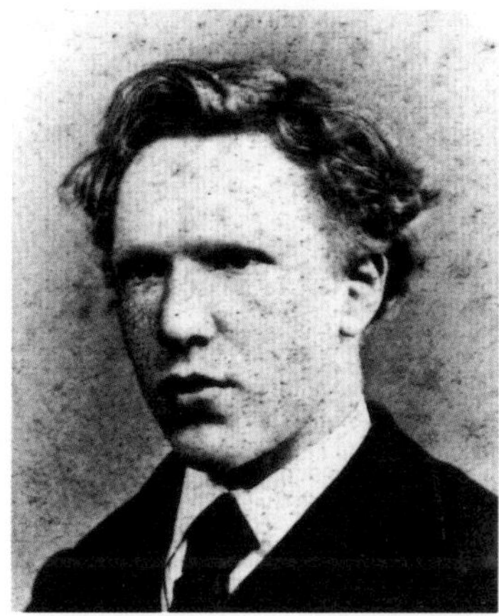

Vincent at age nineteen

KEY

1 ZUNDERT
2 ZEVENBERGEN
3 TILBURG
4 THE HAGUE
5 PARIS
6 LONDON
7 HELVOIRT
8 ETTEN
9 RAMSGATE
10 ISLEWORTH
11 DORDRECHT
12 AMSTERDAM
13 BRUSSELS
14 BORINAGE
15 DRENTHE
16 NUENEN
17 ANTWERP
18 ARLES
19 SAINT REMY
20 AUVERS

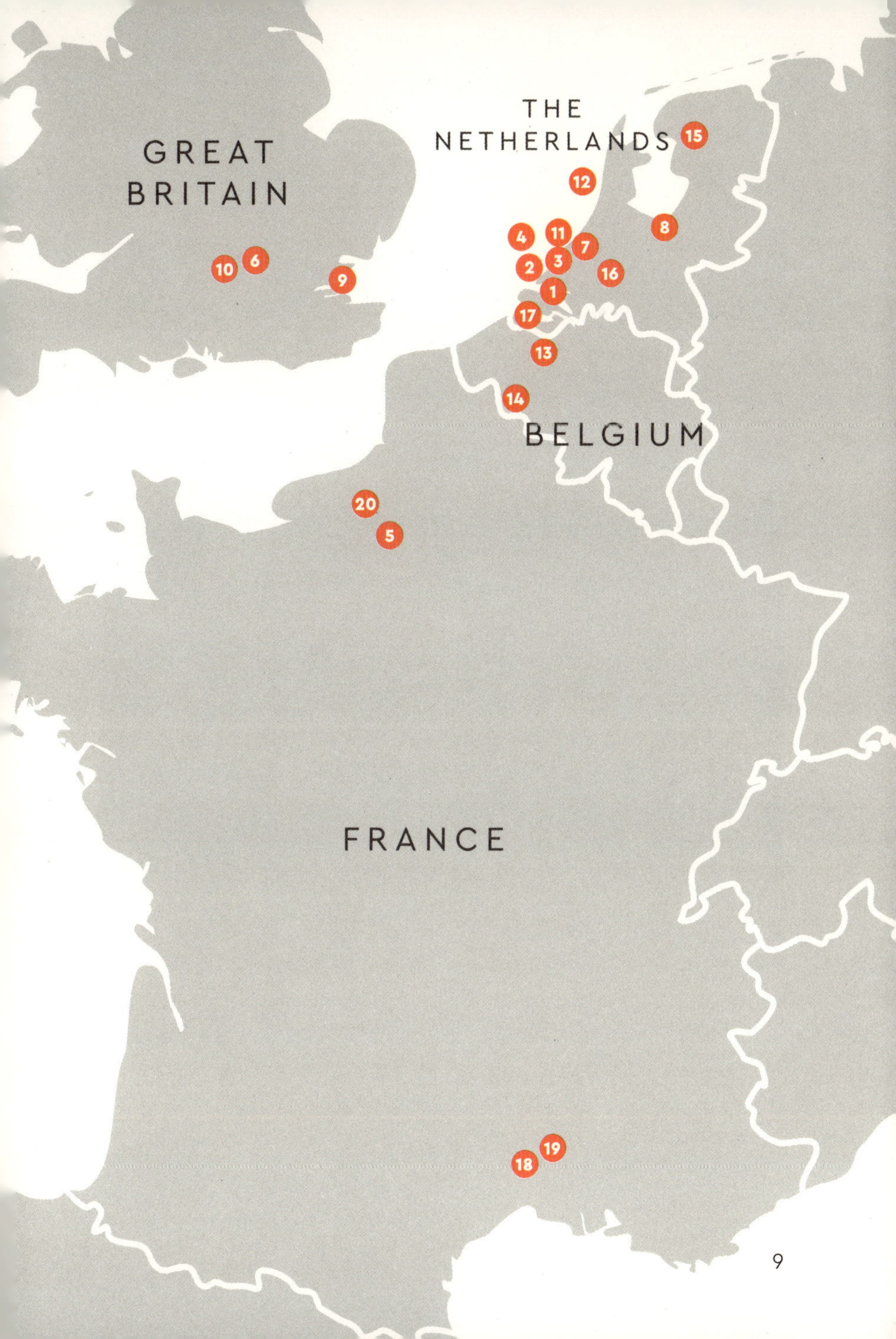

GREAT BRITAIN
THE NETHERLANDS
BELGIUM
FRANCE

ZUNDERT, in the mid-nineteenth century, was a small, country village in the Dutch province of North Brabant near the Belgian border. Predominantly Catholic, its people were devoted to their faith after years of religious conflict. Theodorus van Gogh, a minister in the Dutch Reformed Church, was well loved by his minority congregation. Together with his wife they presented a picture of social conformity and respectability, which they were eager to maintain.

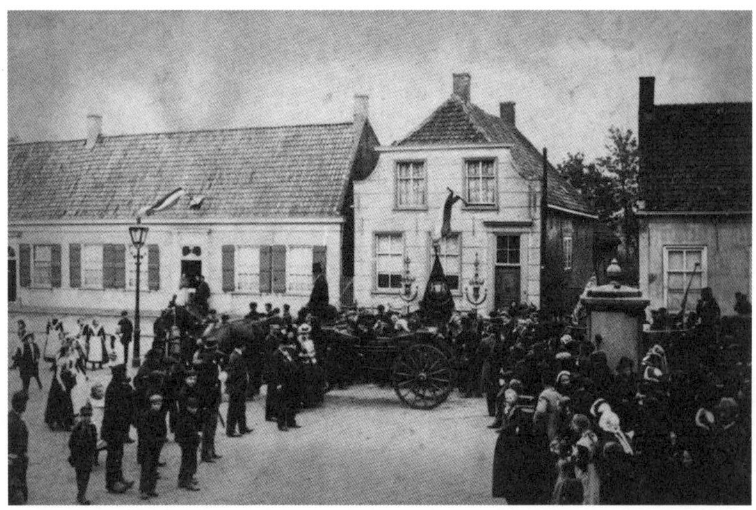

*Photo of Vincent's birthplace
and childhood home.*

Their home, the parsonage, overlooked Zundert's busy central square that was dominated by a large town hall. Vincent was born here in 1853 and was followed by three younger sisters and two brothers.

Discipline was strict in the home, yet young Vincent played freely with his siblings in a flower-filled garden carefully tended by his mother. As he grew older he preferred to be alone. Beyond the garden gate were heathland and moors, wheatfields and creeks. Here, wild life provided him with specimens for a collection – eggs and nests, flowers and beetles. Armed with a net and a bottle, he liked to wander off in search of water insects. He took his creatures home and meticulously stored them in small, paper-lined boxes, carefully categorising them with their correct Latin names. Out in the wide countryside Vincent was free – away from authority and with no demands made of him. Nature was a wonderful companion.

School was less fulfilling. Vincent attended the over-crowded Zundert school on the other side of the square. Here he was discontented and his parents felt it better he remained at home with a governess to study a religious-based curriculum. This also did not prove suitable for Vincent and it was decided he would do better at a boarding school in **ZEVENBERGEN,** 20km from Zundert.

He never forgot his arrival there, aged eleven, and recalled it later when he was an adult.

"It was an autumn day and I stood on the front steps of Mr Provily's school, watching the carriage drive away that Pa and Ma rode home in. One could see that yellow carriage in the distance on the long road – wet after the rain, with thin trees on either side – running through the meadows. The grey sky above it all was reflected in the puddles. And around a fortnight later I was standing one evening in a corner of the playground when they came to tell me that someone was asking after me, and I knew who it was and a moment later I flung my arms round Father's neck.... Between that moment and today are years of pilgrimage."

After only two years he left, but it was not to return home. Another boarding school was found for him, 40km from Zundert in **TILBERG.**

The King William II secondary school was a large, impressive building that was once intended to be a royal palace, although the king for whom it was built had died before its completion. Vincent attained good results there, especially in French, German and English. At the end of the school day he watched his fellow pupils return to their homes while he walked back to his lodgings.

The school at Tilburg was fortunate in having Constantin Huysmans, an established landscape painter, as an art teacher. He encouraged drawing and copying in his classes, but Vincent claimed he learned absolutely nothing there. At the age of fifteen, before completing his education, Vincent left, never to return.

At home the outlook for Vincent's future now was foremost in his parents' thoughts. He required some purpose in an environment that would see him settled in a secure and respectable career. The perfect answer lay in the art dealing business that was closely connected to the family. When he was sixteen, Vincent moved to The Hague to become a junior clerk at Goupil & Cie's art gallery.

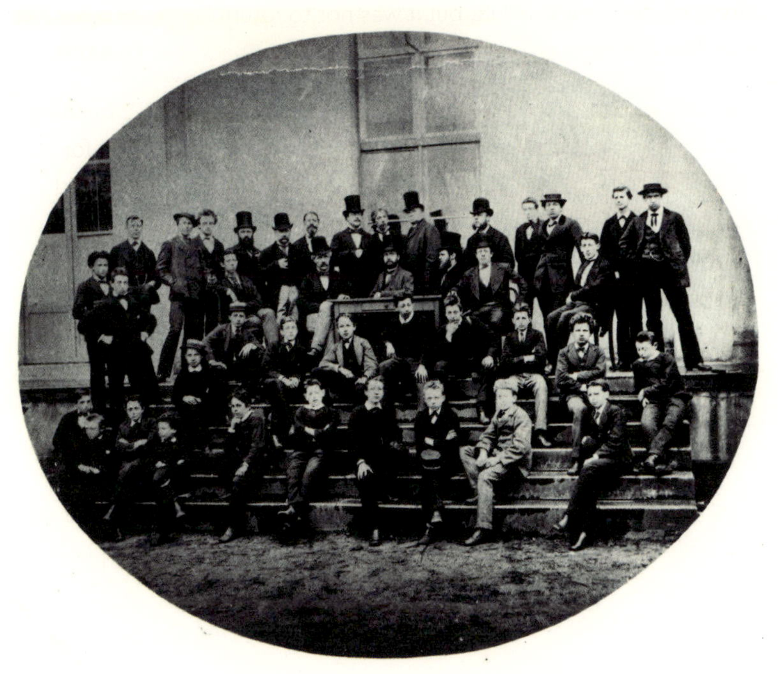

Tilburg School with Van Gogh third
person from the right in front row

THE HAGUE, a large, bustling city at the edge of the sea, is 90km from Zundert, the furthest Vincent had ever been. When his father left him there, he hoped his son would now embark on a period of steady, long-term employment.

Vincent was the youngest of two apprentices working beneath the manager, Hermanus Tersteeg (1845–1927). His job was to handle paintings and prints that were kept in vast stockrooms. These he mounted and packed for despatch. At auctions, he was allowed to bid on behalf of customers. Also at the gallery was a whole range of artists' materials for sale.

Through the many popular reproductions he discovered, Vincent became familiar with some of the best-known names in art. His interest in their work prompted him to visit other galleries and collections in Brussels, Antwerp and Amsterdam. He discovered artists of the Golden Era of Dutch painting and also learned of a contemporary group of painters known as The Hague School.

Prospective buyers at the gallery sat in elegant, beautifully furnished rooms where they could survey many paintings that hung on its walls. Eventually, Vincent was allowed to manage sales himself and in this congenial environment it seemed he had settled down.

Outside work, he stayed with a couple who took in lodgers, but despite those within reach at The Hague, including family members, Vincent was not one to mix easily. He preferred to be alone, to walk on the windy seashore nearby or to devour his favourite books.

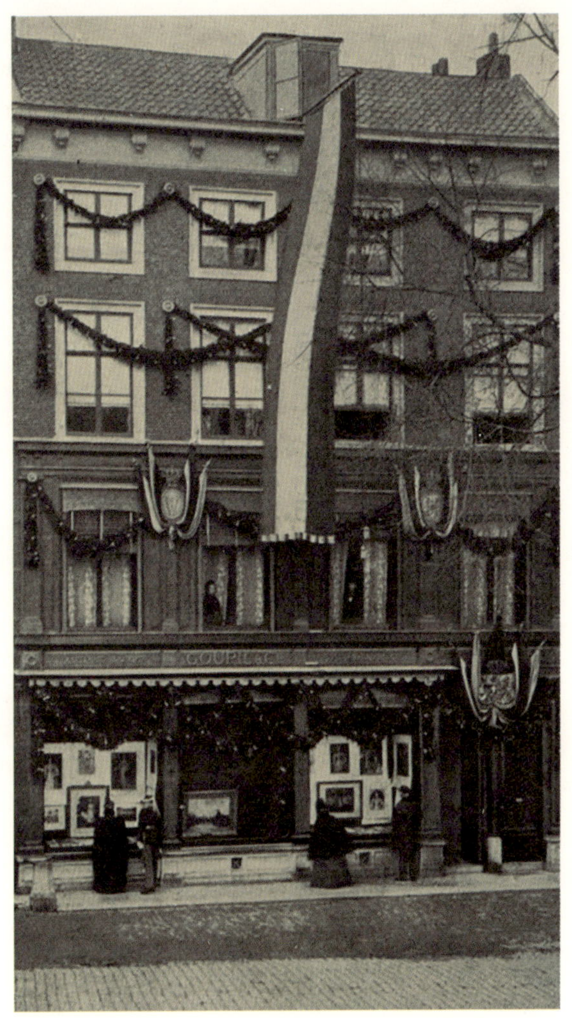

Goupil Gallery,
The Hague

In August 1872, his fifteen-year old brother Theo came to see him. This was a welcome visit, as he loved Theo's company. After he left Vincent began to write to Theo, an occupation that would last his entire life.

"I missed you the first few days, and it was strange for me not to find you when I came home in the afternoon. We spent some pleasant days together, and actually did go for some walks and see a thing or two whenever we had the chance."

Later, Theo also joined the company at its Brussels branch. Vincent warned him that life away from home was strange, but he should keep positive.

"I'm really very happy that you're also part of this firm. It's such a fine firm, the longer one is part of it the more enthusiastic one becomes."

The two older Van Gogh brothers now held jobs that promised greater prospects in the future. However, Vincent was considered unsuitable for the job. Rather than dismiss him entirely, he was allowed to remain in the company and take up a post at the recently opened London branch. Before leaving, he made sketches of familiar spots in The Hague that could serve as reminders of his time there.

The drawings show rural tracks and canal paths where he had liked to walk alone or with Theo – but without any people. Only in street scenes did he add a few passers-by. In a few simple lines he drew typical features of the urban scenes – buildings, lamp-posts, railings, an empty bench. Vincent's recording of specific places had begun.

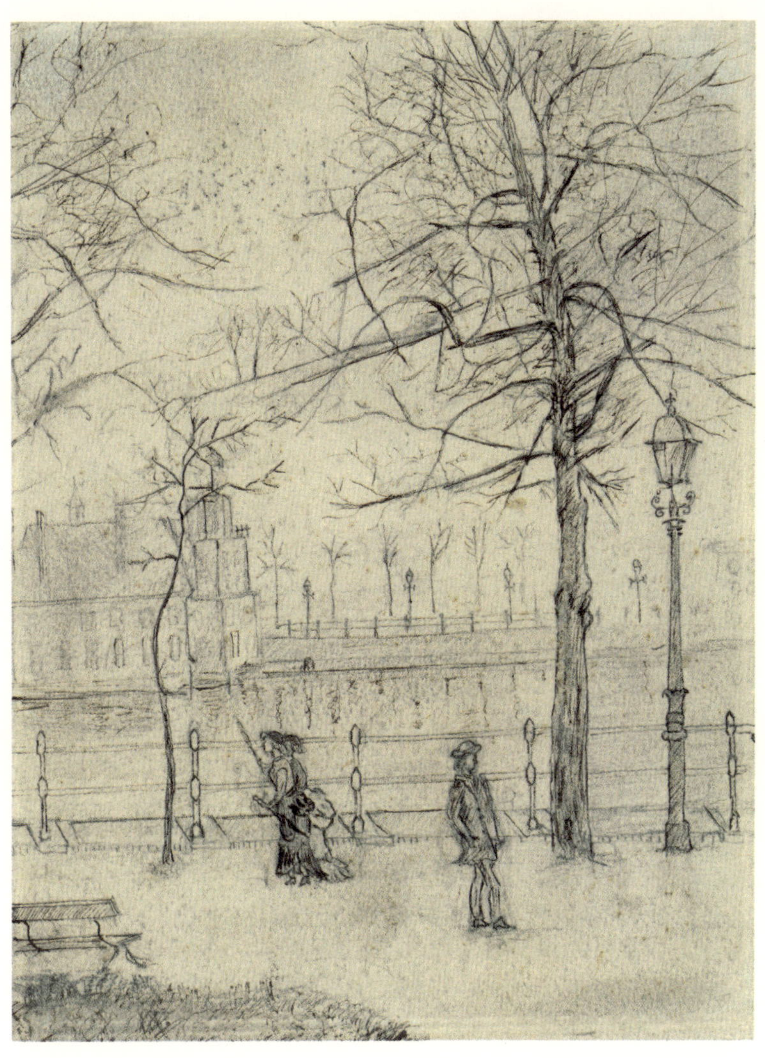

Lange vijverberg, The Hague

On his way to England, Vincent had thought to visit Theo in Brussels but instead paused in **PARIS.** Here his Uncle Cent, the art dealer, entertained him. For a brief week, Vincent was swept up into an unfamiliar and sophisticated world, and he made a point of seeing the best exhibitions.

"I spent some very pleasant days in Paris and, as you can imagine, very much enjoyed all the beautiful things I saw at the exhibition and in the Louvre and the Luxembourg. The Paris branch is splendid and much larger than I'd imagined...."

He visited the Salon, the annual exhibition venue where living artists gained recognition. For him, to become a painter did not even enter his thoughts.

....

After Paris, **LONDON** was something of a shock. A vast city, teeming with people, London spread itself untidily beyond a wide river of impenetrable mists. Vincent found it very expensive.

He arrived in England in the early summer of 1873 and found a quiet place to stay south of the river, where he admired the 'Gothic' features of its villas, so suited to Victorian taste. His fellow lodgers were Germans whose cheerful company he enjoyed in the evenings when they sang round a piano. On his bedroom walls he hung favourite prints that he had brought with him from The Hague.

The London branch of Goupil & Cie was at 17 Southampton Street, close to the Covent Garden market and a fair walk from his lodgings.

It was not yet a gallery but served as an outlet for the wholesale trade of the company's reproductions. Writing to Theo, Vincent thought of his previous post with a hint of nostalgia.

"Write to me especially about the paintings you've seen recently, and also whether anything new has been published in the way of etchings or lithographs. You must keep me well informed about this, because here I don't see much in that genre, as the firm here is just a stockroom."

Although the move felt like involuntary exile to a foreign country, Vincent remained positive. He was adept at improving his grasp of the English language, although his accent was strong. In his spare time he visited London's art galleries. On one occasion, not long after he had arrived, he was thrilled to go into the Surrey countryside with his director, Mr Obach. Finishing work at 6.00pm, in summer daylight, gave him time to make many discoveries out of doors.

"Everywhere one sees splendid parks with tall trees and shrubs, where one is allowed to walk. During the Whitsun holiday I also took a nice trip with those Germans, but those gentlemen spend a great deal of money and I shan't go out with them any more."

At the end of the summer, to make some savings, he moved to 87 Hackford Road, a terraced house in Brixton that gave him a shorter walk to work.

"I now have a room, as I've long been wishing, without sloping beams and without blue wallpaper with a green border. It's a very diverting household where I am now, in which they run a school for little boys."

His new landlady was a widow, Ursula Loyer, whose nineteen-year-old daughter, Eugenie, ran the school. Vincent enjoyed their company. When he returned to his lodgings he felt he had found a new family, as Eugenie was like a sister to him. At Christmas he was received at Mr Obach's home, where he was thrilled to share the season's traditions in an English household. By the New Year he was able to say he was perfectly content.

"Always walking a lot and loving nature, for that's the real way to learn and to understand art better and better. Painters understand nature and love it, and teach us to see."

When he took his pencils and chalk to the other side of the road from his lodgings, Vincent looked hard and created his first real portrait of a building. With careful precision, line by line, he drew the rectangular windows, the iron fence, the lamp-post that marked the corner of the road. Every chimney pot is visible. Tiles on the steeply sloping roofs are drawn with the same detail as bricks on the nearby wall. The terrace takes centre stage, cradled by the shape of the pavement.

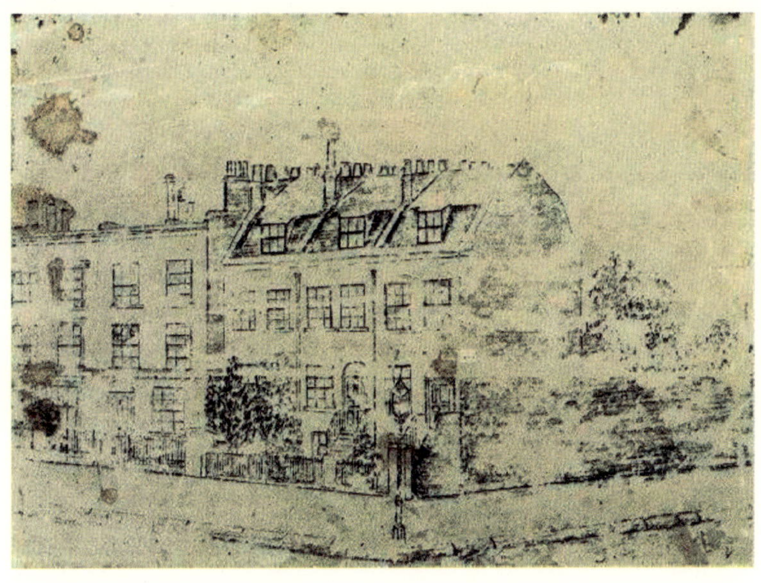

Hackford Road, Brixton, 1873

At his work, the company expanded to include paintings and drawings for sale. This encouraged Vincent and by January 1874 he was able to express a real enjoyment of his life.

"Things are going well for me here, I have a wonderful home and it's a great pleasure for me to observe London and the English way of life and the English themselves, and I also have nature and art and poetry, and if that isn't enough, what is? Yet I haven't forgotten Holland, and especially The Hague and Brabant."

When Anna, the eldest of his sisters, left school, Vincent suggested
she should come to London to find work. Mrs Loyer was happy to
offer Anna a room and looked forward to meeting her. In July, Vincent
travelled to Holland to fetch Anna back. His family had now moved to
a new home and he made sketches of this as well as the paths nearby
where he walked. 'Vincent made many beautiful little drawings,' his
mother wrote to Theo, 'including one for us that he's taken with him
to frame and will then return to us....'

Anna's presence in London reminded Vincent of past times at
home that he always missed. Fortunately, his sister shared his
interest in art and accompanied him on the walks he loved to take.
However, in August both Vincent and Anna left Hackford Road under
circumstances that suggest his behaviour at the Loyers' home was
inappropriate. Had he hoped for more than the sister and brother
relationship with Eugenie – and been refused?

Vincent and Theo wrote at length to each other, especially about
their respective relationships with women. They discussed the nature
of love – that it was possible to have a pure soul and impure body at
the same time. Vincent drew his brother's attention to the writings of
Michelet, the French historian whose daring book L'Amour (1859) lay
emphasis on the physical life of women.

**"A book like that at least teaches one to see that there's a lot more
to love than people usually think."**

Vincent and Anna remained south of the river when they moved to
the home of Mr and Mrs John Parker, a house overgrown with ivy at
395 Kennington Road. Soon afterwards Anna found a job in Welwyn,
north of London, and Vincent was once more alone. Because of his
tendency towards melancholy, his mother feared for his health but
was glad he had left the Loyers': '... there were too many secrets there
and no family like ordinary people'.

Anna wrote about 'a fit of pique' and their mother complained,
'Our Vincent cannot help but feel unhappy now. He has strayed
from the true path, to which alone our blessed Lord attaches
happiness and the joy of living.' As months passed, Vincent's silence
caused mounting fears back in Holland and his family questioned
his behaviour. At work it was decided he should be transferred,
temporarily, to Paris.

The Van Gogh family had moved from Zundert to **HELVOIRT,** another
village in need of Protestant pastoral care. At Christmas the family
were reunited once more. On one of their walks together, Vincent and
Theo went out into the snow and watched the moon rise. The winter
landscape thrilled Vincent. On another very cold evening he rode in
an open cart on a slippery road and noticed dark houses with snow-
covered roofs.

"Brabant is indeed Brabant, and the Mother country is indeed the mother country, and the lands where one is a stranger are the lands where one is a stranger. And how friendly Helvoirt looked that evening, and the lights in the village and the tower between the snow-covered poplars, seen from a distance on the road...."

In May 1875 Vincent left the company's London branch definitively to return to the French capital. Paris had witnessed an astonishing event in the world of art. The previous year a group of artists had mounted their own exhibition, away from the conventional Salon, revealing their distaste for the official selection system. They called themselves the Société Anonyme des Artistes, Peintres, Sculpters et Graveurs. Their works caused a critical stir and the name 'Impressionists' was coined as a derogatory description of their style of painting.

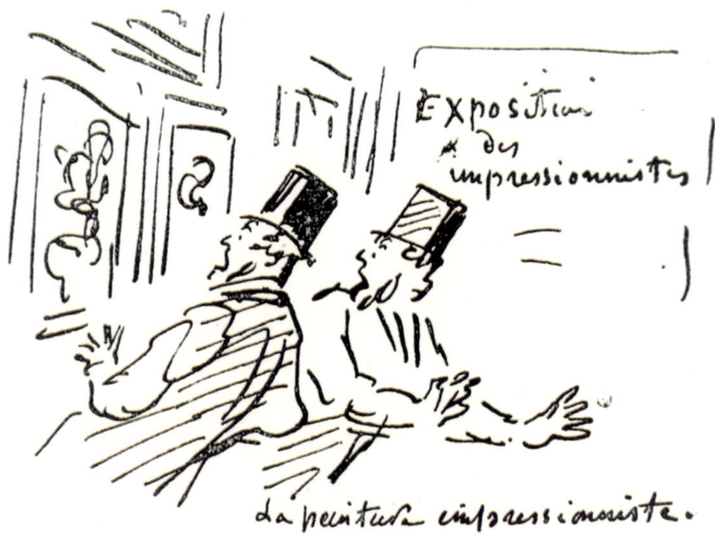

Contemporary cartoon

SOCIETE' ANONYME

DES ARTISTES, PEINTRES, SCULPTERS, GRAVEURS, ETC

PREMIERE

EXPOSITION

1874

35, Boulevard des Capucines, 35

CATALOGUE

Prix : 50 centimes

L'Exposition est ouverte du 15 avril au 15 mai 1874,
de 10 heures du matin a 6 h. du soir et de 8 h. a 10 heures du soir
PRIX D'ENTREE : I FRANC

PARIS
IMPRIMERIE ALCAN-LEVY
61, RUE DE LAFAYETTE

.

1874

Catalogue of the 1874 'Impressionist' exhibition

Vincent now worked at the rue Chaptal, one of several Goupil & Cie premises in Paris. His keen knowledge of prints and paintings gave him a preference for old masters and more popular artists, especially the Barbizon school, a group who had recently lived near the Forest of Fontainebleau. A new railway line from Paris had connected them to a town near the forest. Jean-Baptiste-Camille Corot (1796–1875), Jean-François Millet (1814–75), Charles-François Daubigny (1817–78) and Henri Julien Félix Rousseau (1844–1910) had all spent long periods in the village of Barbizon. Their work revealed a romantic response to the natural world of village and forest, and they encouraged painting out of doors. Vincent particularly liked the work of Millet and found his images of peasant life rich, poetic and moving. He virtually ignored the Impressionists.

He rented a small room in a house on the northern edge of Paris. Montmartre was a high hillside – named as the Mount of Mars in ancient times – that looked out on the city below. The gallery was not far to walk, at the bottom of the hill. Soon after settling in, Vincent gave Theo a full list of the prints he had pinned to his wall. These included Ruisdael and Rembrandt, his Dutch compatriots, and a large selection of Barbizon scenes.

The brothers exchanged not only news of art but they described their working conditions. By late September, however, Vincent's tone was more preaching than brotherly.

"Feeling, even a fine feeling, for the beauties of nature is not the same as religious feeling, although I believe that the two are closely connected. The same is true of a feeling for art.... Nearly everyone has a feeling for nature, some more than others but there are few who feel that God is a spirit and they that worship Him must worship him in spirit and in truth."

On Sundays Vincent regularly attended church, hoping to be inspired by the sermons he heard. Religion was becoming a personal, urgent need.

At his lodgings he made a new friend, a young Englishman, Harry Gladwell (1857–1927), who also worked at Goupil & Cie. Harry had never been away from his family before and was homesick for London. Vincent, who knew London well, took Harry under his wing. They walked home together and ate in Vincent's room (their 'cabin'). As winter approached they sat next to a cosy stove while Vincent read the Bible aloud – he intended to cover the entire book over the coming months. This room, with Harry as a friend, became a haven. In it they even encouraged the company of a mouse they had spied by giving it morsels of bread.

Vincent claimed Harry had an *'unworthy (though noble) yearning for his father and home'*, a comment reflecting his own suppressed feelings that were difficult to overcome. In his letters Vincent described Harry's comic looks, but his own were hardly reassuring. His social awkwardness made him nervous, his red hair was unkempt and his pale eyes often seemed fixed in expression. More significantly, his manner to the customers was often impolite.

By the end of the year it was thought the print dealing business
was no longer suitable for Vincent. At Christmas, when he loved to
be at home, he caused increasing concern for his family. His father
wrote to Theo, 'What will happen to Vincent we do not know yet.
He is certainly not happy. I believe it is not the right place for him
there.' After six years of working for the prestigious firm with its family
connections, his achievement amounted to nothing. Theo, meanwhile,
had steadily gained promotion, had been given a rise in salary and
had the family's full-blown praise.

Vincent returned to Paris in the New Year, soon to be dismissed. He
was told he should never have taken the Christmas break without
formal permission. Determined to go his own way, he had overlooked
such formalities. During the following months, as he worked out his
leave, he applied for positions in England. He now chose to turn his
back on the commercial world of art, but already his experience had
given him a profound appreciation of the art itself.

The parsonage in the village of **ETTEN,** not far from Zundert, had
been the Van Gogh family home since their move there in October
1875. When Vincent arrived in April, he was met with mixed feelings
of disappointment and hope. Would his next move prove more
rewarding than the past year's trials?

Vincent's need of home was strengthened by his failure in work. Once
again he made a record of a place important to him – the new house
and its nearby church. The parsonage is drawn with precision and
clarity. Window frames and their curtains are carefully observed, as

are the church spire and the trees' early spring branches. Fine lines enclose the buildings. Vincent detailed every post of the secure fence that fronted the parsonage.

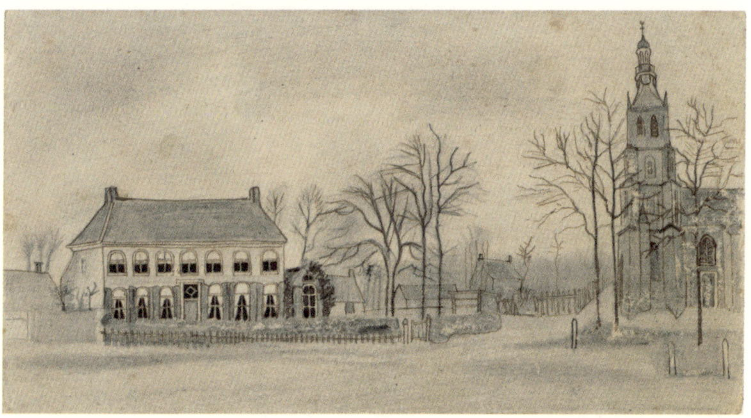

Vicarage and church at Etten, 1876

Before leaving Paris, he had found work as a teacher at a school in England. Here was a new start that might provide him with more fulfilment. However, leaving home was a difficult experience. While he was on the train, having just said goodbye, he wrote to his parents of the unhappiness the wrench caused him.

*"We want to stay together today. Which would be better, the joy of seeing
each other again or the sadness of parting? We've often parted from each
other already, though this time there was more sorrow than before, on
both sides, but courage as well, from the firmer faith in, and greater need
for, blessing. And wasn't it as though nature sympathised with us? It was so
grey and rather dismal a couple of hours ago...."*

The train took him past Zevenbergen, where he remembered that
earlier parting, when as a young boy he was left alone at school. As he
sailed away from Holland he stayed on deck to watch his homeland
disappear. However, once he was back on land, he was thrilled by the
sight of the English countryside.

*"The next morning in the train from Harwich to London it was beautiful to
see in the morning twilight the black fields and green pastures with sheep
and lambs, and here and there a hedge of thorn-bushes and a few large
oak trees with dark branches and grey, moss-covered trunks. The blue twilit
sky, still with a few stars, and a bank of grey clouds above the horizon. Even
before the sun rose I heard a lark."*

Nature consoled and encouraged him. Now, when he confronted fine
scenery, he saw it with the eyes of a painter.

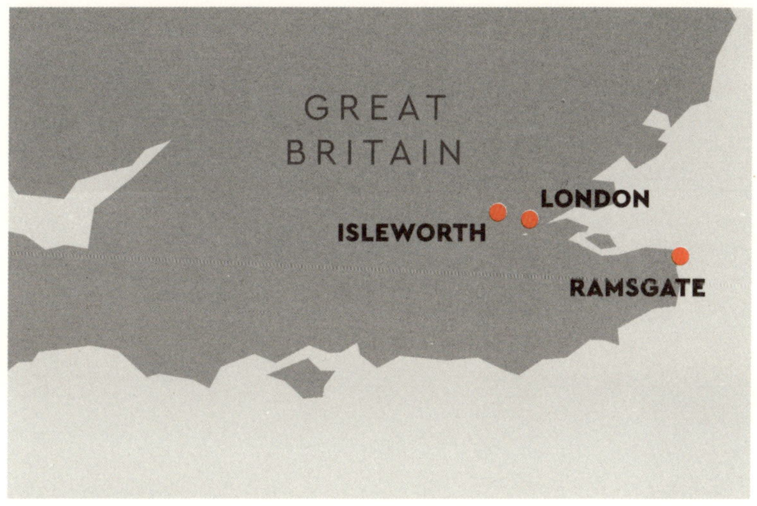

Among the many books that Vincent read, he greatly admired the works of George Eliot and Charles Dickens, with their emphasis on social concerns. The school in **RAMSGATE,** where he took up his first teaching post, was not unlike a Dickensian institution. Twenty-four boys between the ages of ten and fourteen boarded at the home of Mr Stokes (who, he noted, was large with a bald head and whiskers). When he attended the nearby church, Vincent saw a notice that encouraged him, 'Lo, I am with you always, even unto the end of the world'. For the present, such religious phrases might help him on his way. He often walked along the seafront, sometimes with a group of boys if they were in his charge. His teaching duties varied widely, but he doubted the boys would pay him their attention.

Early during his time there, Vincent learned that the school was
soon to move closer to London. Until then he looked carefully at his
surroundings – the weather at all times of the day, the night sky with
a star, the nearby fields and a distant landscape. In one letter he made
a brief sketch of a different kind of scene that moved him.

"Herewith a little drawing of the view from the school window where the
boys stand and watch their parents going back to the station after a visit.
Many a boy will never forget the view from that window...."

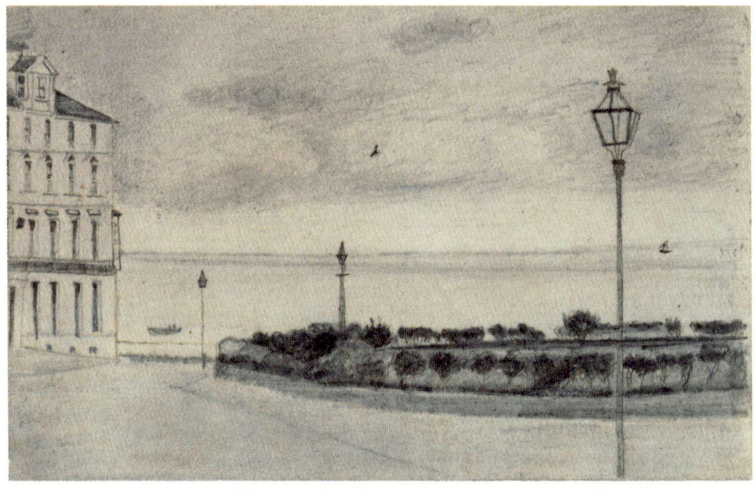

Royal Road, Ramsgate, 1876

His linear style recorded the stark horizontal of the edge of the road
and the verticals on the building opposite, matched by isolated lamp-
posts. A wide, empty foreground remains empty, devoid of life.

Life in the school, especially for the boys, was not easy. Vincent was
quick to describe it in a letter to Theo.

*"Another extraordinary place is the room with a rotten floor where there are
six basins at which they wash themselves, with only a feeble light falling
onto the washstand through a window with broken panes. It's quite a
melancholy sight, to be sure. How I'd like to spend or to have spent a winter
with them, to know what it's like. The youngsters are making an oil stain on
your little drawing, forgive them."*

When Vincent visited his sister, Anna, and walked an astonishing
distance from Ramsgate to Welwyn, he considered the poor deal he
received from Mr Stokes. Board and lodging, but no salary, was his
only payment. He began to see himself suited to work with the poor
and to fill a role somewhere between schoolmaster and missionary.
A note to a prospective employer stated his hopes for yet another
new start.

*"Although I have not been trained for the church, perhaps my past life of
travelling, living in various countries, associating with a variety of people,
rich and poor, religious and not religious, working at a variety of jobs, days
of manual labour in between days of office work, etc. perhaps also my
speaking various languages, will compensate in part for my lack of formal
training...."*

Mr Stokes' establishment moved to **ISLEWORTH,** on London's western fringe. Here, after a few days, Vincent found alternative employment. This was at another school run by the Rev. Thomas Slade-Jones. He lived with the headmaster's large family in a fine, three-storey house, which had a playground for the schoolboys and a garden.

Vincent's new employer engaged him to teach and take on varied clerical duties, both in and out of school. Soon he became his assistant preacher, despite his inexperience. Hours at work did not prevent his wide programme of reading and on his upper-storey bedroom walls he hung more reproductions that recalled his attachment to art. Wherever he lodged this display of favourite prints always helped to settle him.

To preach God's word was Vincent's new vocation.

"Who sees, when the first life, the life of childhood and adolescence, that life of joy in the world and vanity reluctantly withers, and it will wither, even as the blossom falls from the trees, that then another life shoots up vigorously, the life of the love of Christ...."

Vincent became familiar with several non-conformist churches in the area. He prepared services, taught Sunday school classes and occasionally led evening prayer. In a letter to Theo, he drew two of these churches in the linear style he had already established that enabled him to record their structure precisely.

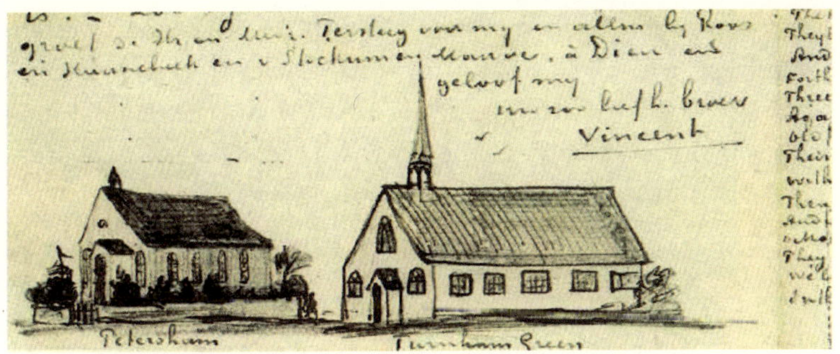

Churches at Turnham Green and Petersham, 1876

On 29 October 1876, Vincent delivered his first sermon at the Wesleyan Methodist Church in Richmond. Proudly, he wrote to Theo describing the lovely walk he took along the Thames and the red-roofed houses he saw on his way to the church. When he addressed the congregation he felt he had emerged from a dark underground vault into friendly daylight. He encouraged Theo to have faith when moments of difficulties arose. At the end of his letter he included the script of his sermon – its passionate tone revealing his idea that as human beings we are strangers on the earth, wandering on troubled seas.

"Our life, we might compare to a journey, we go from the place where we were born to a far off haven. Our earlier life might be compared to sailing on a river, but very soon the waves become higher, the wind more violent, we are at sea almost before we are aware or it – and the prayer from the heart ariseth to God: Protect me o God, for my boat is so small and Thy sea is so great."

Vincent's calling did not deflect his awareness of the children at the school, many of whom came from impoverished homes. His own experiences of boarding were not forgotten and he was moved by their common situation. His rapport with youngsters was naturally warm. He watched them closely. Sometimes when out together, he told them Hans Christian Andersen's tales.

"How I wish you could see the playground now, and the garden behind it, in the twilight, inside the school the gas lamps flicker and one hears the congenial sound of the boys learning their lessons, from time to time one of them starts humming a snatch of melody from some hymn or other...."

One of his more disagreeable tasks was to seek out the homes of those families who could not afford the school fees. With his map of London to assist him, he discovered their addresses in new areas he had never seen, but was soon made uncomfortable by his task. They lived in conditions that shocked him. At times he returned to the school with less money than he should have collected. The plight of the poor stirred his religious feeling.

Wherever he walked, Vincent kept his eyes on nature, noticing the seasons' beauty, spreading mists, the colours of leaves or the play of streetlights on dampened pavements. He found time to walk long distances and once left Isleworth at four in the morning to go to Hyde Park, to Westminster, to Clapham and to visit the Loyers. Frequently he headed for Lewisham when his old friend Harry Gladwell was back from Paris, visiting his family. The homes of these old acquaintances were a different kind of landmark on his London map where he found companionship and a closeness that resembled family life.

However, nothing matched the profound joy he knew at his own home, especially at Christmas. When he next returned to Etten he described his unsatisfactory London life and it was suggested he might try a new job in Holland. The pay would be better than a schoolteacher's and he would live nearer to home than he had done in years. On New Year's Eve 1876, he announced the new plan to Theo.

"There are many things that make It desirable, first and foremost my being back in Holland near Pa and Ma, and also you and the others. Moreover, the salary would certainly be a little better than with Mr Jones, and especially with an eye to later, when a man has need of more, one is obliged to think of such things.... The change means that now, instead of teaching those boys, I'll be working in a bookshop."

His teaching career had lasted eight months.

....

DORDRECHT was a thriving coastal city formed into an island during a flood in the fifteenth century. When Vincent arrived to take up his new position, he eagerly sought the work of its native painters. Once he had found lodgings, he pinned more prints on the walls.

"The window of my room looks out over gardens with pine trees and poplars, etc. and the back of old houses, including a large one covered with ivy, 'a strange old plant is the ivy green', said Dickens. There can be something so serious and rather sombre in that view and you should see it with the morning sun on it.... The evening sun went down and was reflected in the water and the windows, throwing a strong golden glow on everything, it was just like a painting by Cuyp."

Blussé and Van Braam booksellers stood in the market square, opposite his lodgings. His working hours at a menial job were extremely long, from 8.00am until midnight. Occasionally, if a customer needed information on prints that were also sold at the shop, Vincent's experience in the art world prompted him to offer his opinion and advice. However, this was not the right work for him. He became seriously depressed.

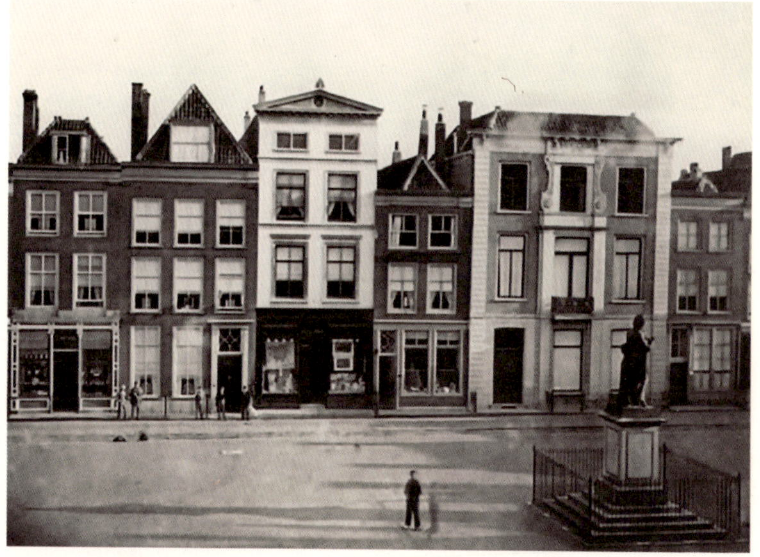

Scheffersplein, Dordrecht market square, 1877
(with the bookshop in middle)

During the night, he spent many hours reading by lamplight while smoking incessantly. Fortunately, his roommate was tolerant, but Vincent's landlord complained of his habits, especially when he drove nails into the walls. He also talked at length, at work and at home, enthusing with passion about his personal convictions. Nothing satisfied the hunger he felt for some kind of religious occupation.

He now showered biblical quotes through the words of his long letters. On Sundays he visited churches of several denominations, eager to hear more sermons. Gradually he became estranged from others as his unkempt appearance baffled them. He began to deny himself food.

Family members were not far away and Vincent and Theo often found each other in their respective cities. Their walks were always comforting. One morning in early April, he set off to go back to Zundert, the place of his childhood. For the last 16km he was on foot.

"It was so beautiful there on the heath, even though it was dark one could make out the heath and the pine-woods and the marshes stretching far and wide, it reminded me of that illustration by Bodmer that's hanging in Pa's study. The sky was grey but the evening star shone through the clouds, and now and then other stars were visible too. It was still very early when I arrived at the cemetery in Zundert, where it was so quiet, I went to have a look at all the old places and paths and waited for the sun to rise."

Returning to his childhood home narrowed the years since his departure. It remained in his memories, which he shared with Theo.

"I was walking alone on that dyke, I thought how good that Dutch soil was, and I felt something akin to 'today it is in mine heart to make a covenant with my God' because memories of times past came back to me, including how often we walked with Pa to Rijsbergen and so on in the last days of February and heard the lark above the black fields with young green wheat, the shimmering blue sky with white clouds above – and then the paved road with beech trees – O Jerusalem Jerusalem! or rather O Zundert O Zundert! Who knows but that we may go walking at the seaside together this summer? We really must remain good friends, Theo, and simply believe in God and trust with that faith of old in Him who is able to do above all that we ask or think – who can say to what heights grace can ascend?"

As his religious fervour grew, Vincent craved a new vocation in the church. At home in Etten the family became fearful once more. Influential uncles were called upon for advice and although his past performances were unimpressive, Vincent's determination to follow in his father's steps – and the obsessional nature this wish had taken – could not be refused. It was pointed out that if he seriously wanted to become a preacher, he would need to train for this vocation.

The family acted as a buttress holding up Vincent's wavering sense of self-worth. He had uncles living in **AMSTERDAM** who adopted different roles for keeping Vincent on his newly chosen path.

Uncle Stricker, a preacher himself, found a tutor to teach Vincent Latin and Greek – preliminaries for a serious study of theology at university. He also undertook to regularly monitor Vincent's progress.

Uncle Jan was a retired Rear Admiral whose lifestyle was one of efficiency and order. He offered Vincent his home. No longer in cheap lodgings, Vincent stayed with this widowed, childless relative in a fine house overlooking Amsterdam's lively dockyards.

His uncles entertained and watched over him. His tutor patiently began their studies but from the start the work was demanding.

"I see that it isn't easy and will no doubt become much more difficult, yet have unfaltering hope that I'll succeed, and I'm also convinced that I'll learn to work by working, and that my work will become better and more substantial. I've already begun studying the Bible, but only in the evenings, when I've finished my work for the day, or early in the morning – after all, that's the most important thing."

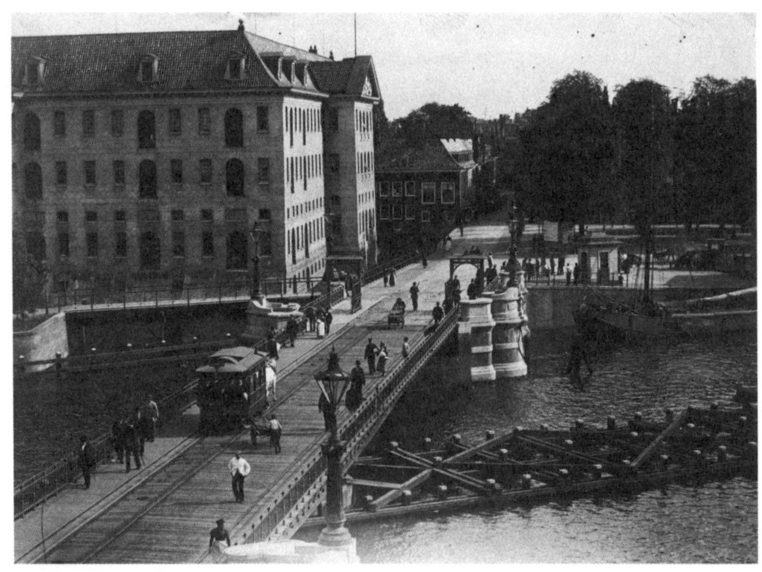

Kattenburgenbrug – the naval dockyard in Amsterdam

From his window Vincent watched the activities of busy, working people in a scene that represented not only the life of the modern city but a reminder of its seafaring history.

"A terrible storm blew up this morning at a quarter to 5, a little while later the first stream of workers came through the gate of the dockyard in the pouring rain. Got up and went into the yard and took a couple of notebooks to the cupola and sat there reading and looking round the whole yard and dock, the poplars and elders and other shrubs were bent by the strong wind, and the rain pelted on the wood-piles and the decks of the ships, sloops.... Again and again one heard thunder and saw lightning, the sky looked like a painting by Ruisdael."

At night his window revealed the bright glare of streetlamps and the sky filled with stars. Each day hé took a long walk and, when time allowed, his most pleasurable occupation was to go further out towards the sea and the country, on the city's outskirts. He longed for the day when his training would be over.

"My head is sometimes numb and is often burning hot, and my thoughts are confused – how shall I ever get all that difficult and detailed study into it?"

Vincent's fervent night-time Bible reading to complement his daily studies became part of an extreme routine, which concerned Uncle Jan. As months went by and he obtained no real pleasure from his studies, he began a course of punishing physical self-abuse, denying himself food and sleeping outside in a shed. He knew he was failing not only his tolerant relatives in the city but also his family at home.

In Etten for Christmas 1877, he kept up a veneer of optimism as he recounted his progress, but family members were not to be fooled. They detected his true mental state. On his return to Amsterdam, Vincent's mood began to descend into severe depression. Only activities outside studying were going to help him. He attended churches and listened to sermons until his urgent need for an occupation that suited his ardent temperament was met by fresh inspiration. Vincent would preach to the poor, working alongside labourers, giving them the comfort of God's words. He would not abandon the calling of religion, but take an alternative route towards it.

Disappointment in Vincent's latest abandoned project was emphasised by Theo's continuing rise in the family firm and a transfer to Paris. Vincent was now twenty-five and had succeeded in nothing.

Eventually, attendance at an evangelical training school in **BRUSSELS** was considered the most practical step forward in his new choice. From home in Etten, his father accompanied him on a new journey.

"We saw the Flemish training college ... one is not even required to complete the training before competing for a place and position as an Evangelist. What is required is the talent to give easy, warm-hearted and popular lectures or speeches to the people, better short and to the point than long and learned."

In the summer of 1878 Vincent moved to Belgium and boarded with a family in Laken, a suburb to the north of Brussels. Another lodger and fellow student, Pieter, was alarmed to witness the strict regime Vincent imposed on himself – he ate little and refused to sleep in a bed, instead preferring a mat on the floor.

In the neighbourhood where he now lived, Vincent discovered a path along the Willebroek Canal. Not far from the dominant site of gasworks were moored barges laden with coal. He was struck by the sight of the poor, whose livelihood was earned through punishing hardship. The rough working café used by miners attracted his eye and he was moved to record it.

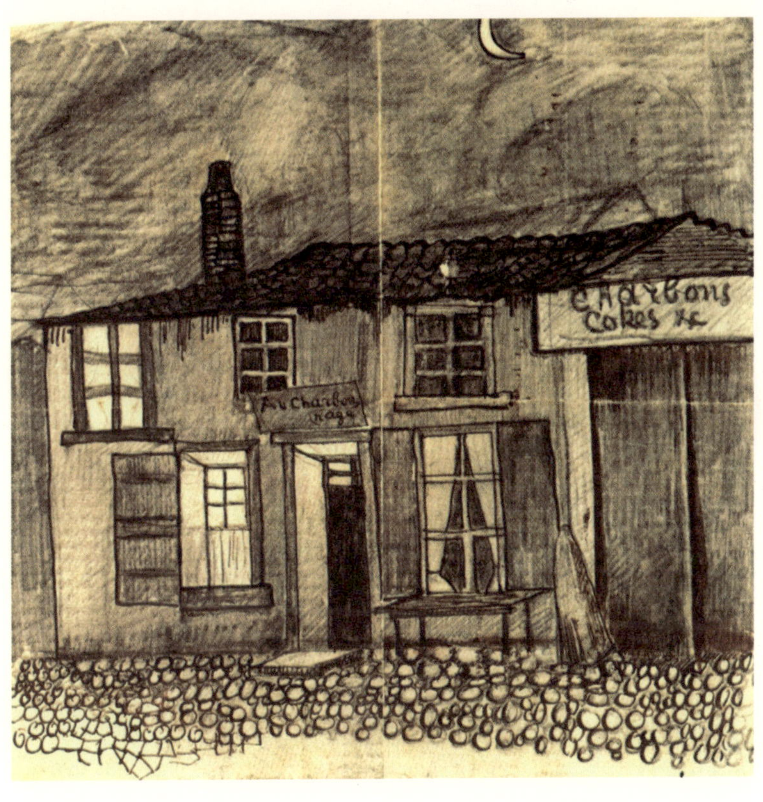

'Au Charbonnage' café, 1878

"That little drawing, Au Charbonnage café, is really nothing special, but the reason I couldn't help making it is because one sees so many coalmen, and they really are a remarkable people. This little house is not far from Trekweg, it's actually a simple inn right next to the big workplace where the workers come in their free time to eat their bread and drink a glass of beer."

Although he claimed it was 'nothing special', he had created a portrait of the characterful building. His linear drawing style faithfully follows the lopsided angles of the café's features and he defines several outlines with ink. Welcoming light shines through the windows, some of which are curtained. Above the shallow, dipped roof a crescent moon hangs in a darkened sky. No person is there but the café is ready to receive thirsty miners once they have crossed a cobbled path to the front door.

After his three-month trial at the school, Vincent was refused further training on financial grounds. Instead, he made the bold decision to head further into Belgium to join the working miners and to preach to them.

Vincent's missionary zeal was not suitable for religion as a formal and demanding profession, but he believed that to preach to impoverished people like himself might provide him with personal fulfilment. A post was found for him in Wasmes, a village in the Belgian mining district known as the **BORINAGE.** Here a six-month trial period began in December 1878.

"As far as I'm concerned, you surely understand that there are no paintings here in the Borinage, that in general they haven't the slightest idea of what a painting is, so it goes without saying that I've seen absolutely nothing in the way of art since my departure from Brussels. But this doesn't mean that this isn't a very special and very picturesque country, everything speaks, as it were, and is full of character."

The 'character' he spoke of was the brooding darkness of this place known as the Black Country. The people who mined here, their horses and their clothes were blackened by soot. The main features on the harsh landscape were buildings attached to the mines – rearing slag-heaps, stark chimneys, pulleys over the pit-heads and, at a short distance, the miners' homes.

"Their houses are usually small and could better be called huts, scattered along the sunken roads and in the wood against the slopes of the hills. One sees moss-covered roofs here and there, and the light shines kindly in the evening through the small-paned windows."

The miners found little 'kindly' in their wretched existence. Vincent hoped to offer them consolation. Although he visited mines, his role of preacher detached him from his flock. His appearance was strange and they could not understand his accent. However, illness was rife in the area and when he visited the sick, he believed he did them good.

"I just visited an old mother in a charcoal-burner's family. She's seriously ill but pious and patient. I read a chapter and prayed with all of them. The people here have something special and appealing because of their simplicity and kind-heartedness, just like the Brabanters in Zundert and Etten."

Vincent had arrived in a land where people had great spiritual needs. His compassionate nature was not enough to help them and his behaviour was unhelpfully eccentric. He was frowned upon with suspicion, even by those less fortunate than himself. At first he lodged with a farmer in Wasmes but he preferred to be on his own. As time moved on, he deliberately denied himself all physical care, refusing food, a bed, even clothing. He slept in a cold, thatched hut – but his belief in his care of others sustained him. When a terrible explosion in one of the mines occurred, Vincent willingly attended the suffering with practical and consoling nursing.

After six months his post was terminated. He was considered lacking in any qualities needed to fulfil the role of evangelist. He did not speak eloquently nor organise meetings where his words could help his listeners. Vincent returned to Brussels. Thanks to his persuasive and sincere wish to return to the Borinage, he found another job, this time in the village of Cuesmes.

When it came to depicting the people with whom he worked, Vincent saw the miners and their family members as 'types', not unlike the characters he found in literature. He cared little for himself, but with no formal contract of work, was more like a wandering tramp than a preacher. Yet he believed he was in the right place. In the Borinage he began to make serious studies of people – usually the miners on their way to work.

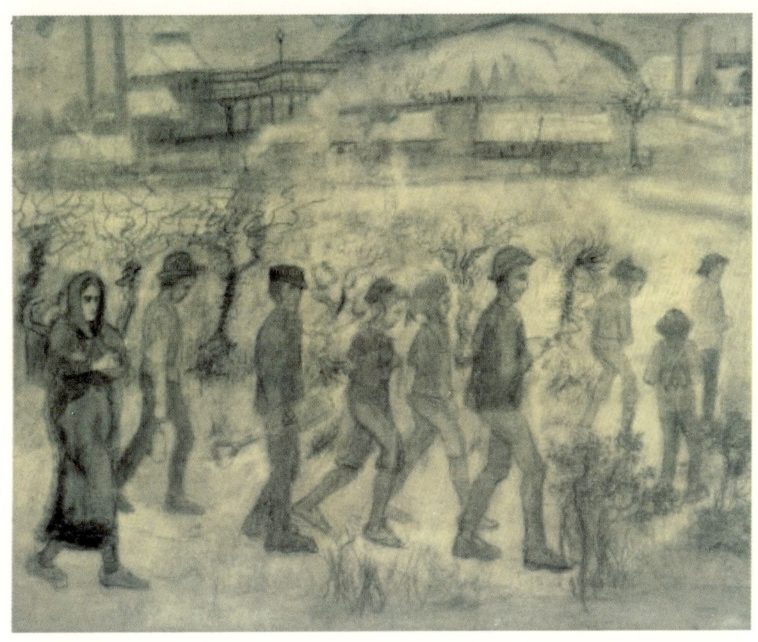

Miners, 1880

"I've done a scratch of miners, male and female thrutchers going to the pit in the morning, in the snow, on a path beside a thorn-hedge; passing shadows, dimly visible in the dusk. In the background, the large mine buildings and the slag heap are becoming indistinct against the sky."

The need to create was unconsciously forming as Vincent persevered
with his personal, obsessive and misplaced mission. At home
the family's concern for him escalated and his father considered
committing him to an asylum. Whole periods of silence followed. In
a moment of nostalgia, Vincent thought of returning to England. For
three days, sleeping rough, he headed towards the French coast. His
observant eye noticed how the sky was clear rather than filled with
smoke. Turning around, he returned to the Borinage like an aimless
wanderer.

He told Theo about the drawings he had done and described the
merit of an artists' manual he used. Books on the various practical
aspects of creating art were now his night-time reading. He studied
prints and made copies of many, especially those by Millet, the
peasant painter of Barbizon. To draw was now his preoccupation.

Further hardship and the unsuitability of his chosen path soon led
him towards a different kind of training – not in the missions of an
evangelical church but in the studios of artists back in Brussels.

*"I couldn't tell you how happy I feel to have taken up drawing again. It had
already been on my mind for a long time, but I always saw the thing as
impossible and beyond my reach. But now, while feeling both my weakness
and my painful dependence in respect of many things, I've recovered my
peace of mind, and my energy is coming back day by day."*

In September 1880 Vincent saw his departure from the Borinage as
another move forward where he took steps towards a more suitable
future. In order to shed his long, mistaken missionary voyage, he
would resurrect himself as an artist.

In Brussels, he found lodgings above a café at 72 boulevard du Midi. Here he continued his usual pattern of study, reading and copying. The image of Millet's sower, whose task was to spread seeds for a future crop, was a relevant and favourite motif. He spruced himself up, ready to approach those people in the city he hoped might prove useful. If he could find an established artist willing to teach him, he would be well on his way.

"Also went to see Mr van Rappard, who now lives at rue Traversière 64, and have spoken to him. He has a fine appearance, I've not seen anything of his work other than a couple of small pen drawings of landscapes. But he lives rather sumptuously and, for financial reasons, I don't know whether he's the person with whom, for instance, I could live and work. But in any case I'll go and see him again. But the impression I got of him was that there appears to be seriousness in him."

Anthon van Rappard (1858–92), younger than Vincent, became a good friend. He was doing well with contemporary subjects in an appealing, painterly style. From an affluent family, he was completely at ease socially. Soon the two men worked side by side in the country. Such closeness was held dear by Vincent, who did not make friends easily. He knew he needed Rappard's instruction to go beyond the stiff, charcoal figures he had done in the Borinage that might not be suitable for sale.

Money was urgently required for his upkeep and for models at Rappard's studio that he now shared. However, when Rappard left Brussels for the summer, Vincent did not care to be alone. He returned to the parsonage at Etten.

"I'm very glad indeed that it's been arranged for me to work here quietly for a while, I hope to make as many studies as I possibly can, for that's the seed from which later drawings will grow."

At home, liberated from mounting financial cares, Vincent went on to the heath in all weathers, seeking to draw the peasants who lived and worked nearby. His subject matter now was close to that of Millet and the painters of the Barbizon school – people of the land, their tools, the meadows, the barns – the entire rural environment of their work. To accommodate his artistic needs, an outbuilding in the parsonage garden was turned into a studio. He attacked his work in long, arduous sessions, not unlike the way he had driven himself as a preacher.

Rappard came to stay for nearly two weeks and provided the kind of company of which Vincent's parents approved. They went on long walks together to study the landscape and the peasants' world. The stimulation Rappard brought Vincent through their preference for the same subjects, as well as his encouragement, was heartening. However, when his friend left, Vincent was once more alone.

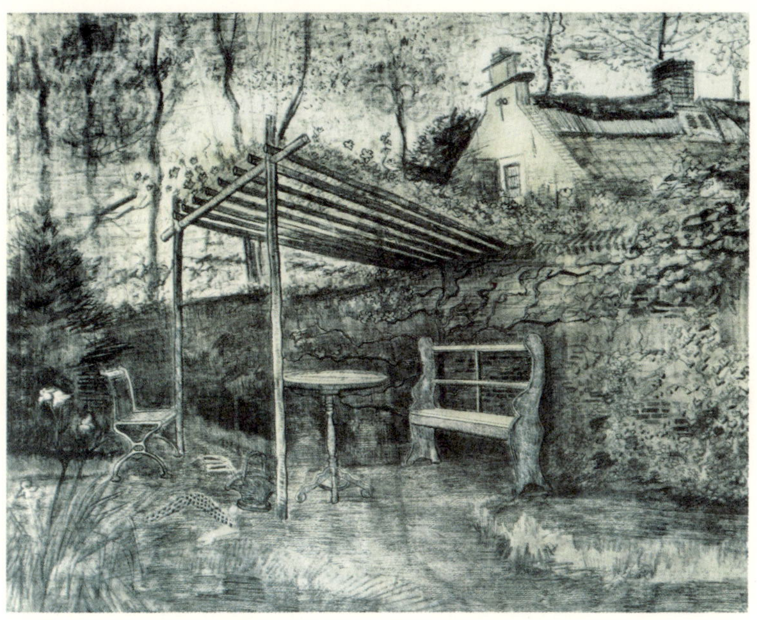

The Garden of the Parsonage with Arbor, 1881

The large drawing he made of the parsonage garden in Etten was an accomplished and finished work of art. It shows a quiet and tranquil corner of a private place. No peasants toil here, nor is there anyone to fill the empty bench and chair beneath the arbour. The whole closely observed scene is suggestive of human presence – and absence.

In August 1881 the family had a visit from Vincent's cousin, Kee Vos, the daughter of Uncle Stricker. Vincent had not seen her for three years, during which time her husband had died, leaving her to bring up her eight-year-old son. Vincent decided he should marry her. With a wife and child he would never be alone, nor would he need to pay for women's company. He could set up a real home of his own and the changed domestic situation would surely further his work.

Kee's immediate shock and refusal did not discourage him. He saw it as another obstacle to overcome. If her rejection was because of his earning capacity, then he would sell his drawings. Vincent took off to The Hague to seek out his cousin by marriage, Anton Mauve (1838–88), a successful artist well known in the city. Mauve lived the perfect life as a married man and a father, and was widely recognised for his work. Vincent was jubilant when Mauve encouraged and advised him to continue drawing but to try different media.

On his way home Vincent paused in the country near Dordrecht to record a group of windmills.

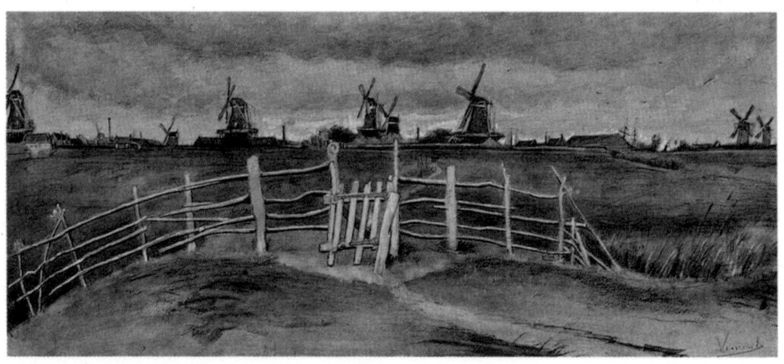

Windmills at Dordrecht, 1881

Across the wide piece of paper his view includes a strategic and picturesque fence that relieves and separates the bare foreground from the rest of the scene. In the distance are windmills, silhouettes against a rain-filled sky. This was his homeland.

Here he took up his preferred themes.

"Diggers, sowers, ploughers, men and women I must now draw constantly. Examine and draw everything that's part of a peasant's life. Just as many others have done and are doing. I'm no longer powerless in the face of nature, as I used to be."

In his letters to Theo he included sketches and explained that any money his brother spent on him would become an investment when at last his drawings were sold. Out in the country, along paths and roads lined with pollard trees, he composed drawings that captured the nature of the flat countryside with its few, striking features.

Kee's refusal of marriage was not forgotten. Now his obsessive nature saw 'Love' as another worthy goal. He hardly knew Kee, nor did he understand the reality of her side of the story. Mistakenly, he dreamed of a time when she would accept him and live with him.

The parsonage was disrupted as Vincent scolded others for their lack of faith in this new, personal project. When his family pointed out his alarming delusion, he turned on them. Gradually he found fault with the Bible, claiming to prefer Michelet, the risqué author of L'Amour. At Christmas the years of struggle, frustration and bitter recrimination grew to a head when he refused to go to church.

*"I was angrier than I ever remember being in my whole life, and I told
Pa plainly that I found the whole system of that religion loathsome, and
precisely because I dwelled on those things too much during a miserable
time in my life I don't want anything more to do with it, and have to guard
against it as against something fatal."*

Vincent's family no longer knew what to do. They had welcomed him home and provided for his needs over many months. The rift between father and son was born of frustration on both sides. Finally, pushed to the limits of tolerance, his father told him to leave. Vincent saw this departure as a second exile from home.

His flight left behind him a house of grief. Ahead were more disruptive battles. He could not easily face opposition to his ideas, which were often unreasonable or distorted. His immediate recourse was a return to The Hague to seek out Mauve, his more gentle relative, friend and fellow artist. Although Vincent found consolation under Mauve's patient encouragement, he later disapproved of his cousin's advice. Mauve suggested he should steer away from figure drawing and work from plaster casts, to better understand the anatomy of the human body. Vincent, who liked to work from real, live people, did not approve of the idea. This provoked their falling out and Vincent went in search of other artists in the city who, like Mauve, were already part of the established Hague School. To work alongside kindred spirits would stave off loneliness.

Mauve had helped him financially and Theo continued to send him money. In January 1882 Vincent moved into his first, independent rooms, sparing no expense on the furnishings.

"It happens to everyone at some point in life that he has to set himself up in his own house, and although at first I couldn't face being in debt, I do feel that it is better this way."

Vincent's studio on the outskirts of The Hague was on the Schenkweg, a partially built-up area, close to the railway. From here he searched for any models who were willing to pose long hours for little pay. These were women of all ages, sometimes with children he had to cajole. Diggers, road-menders, the unemployed who spent daylight hours on the streets searching for a means of sustenance – Vincent asked them all into his studio.

Outside, despite the cold, he worked at these new urban subjects. He frequented the working class area, the Geest, where popular markets were held. At one time he discovered where sewerage pipes were being laid – here were his models at work, in poses not unlike the land-tilling peasants of Millet.

"Struggling on wharves and in alleys and streets and inside houses, waiting rooms, even public houses, that's not a nice job, unless one is an artist. As such one would rather be in the filthiest neighbourhood, provided there's something to draw, than at a tea party with nice ladies."

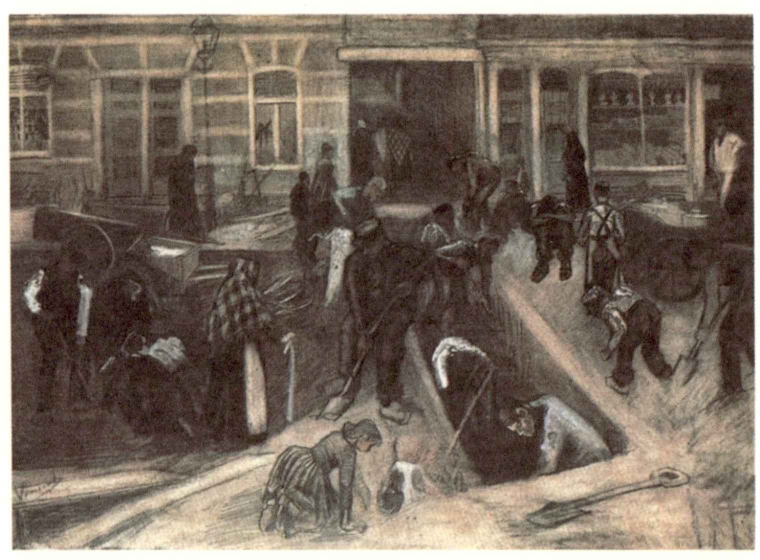

Torn-up Noordstraat with Diggers, 1882

One of his models, Sien Hoornik, was a pregnant prostitute. Vincent met her and her daughter early in 1882. He had always been fond of children and held the image of family life as a sacred ideal. Now he hoped to save Sien from her tragic lifestyle, despite his own meagre livelihood that was entirely dependent on his brother.

"If I don't marry her, it would have been kinder of me not to have taken any interest in her. Yet through this step a gulf opens; I then 'marry beneath my station', as they say, as decisively as I possibly can, but that is not forbidden and not bad, even if the world calls it wrong. My domestic arrangements will be like those in a worker's household."

As he searched to perfect his drawing style, Sien continued to model for him in their home.

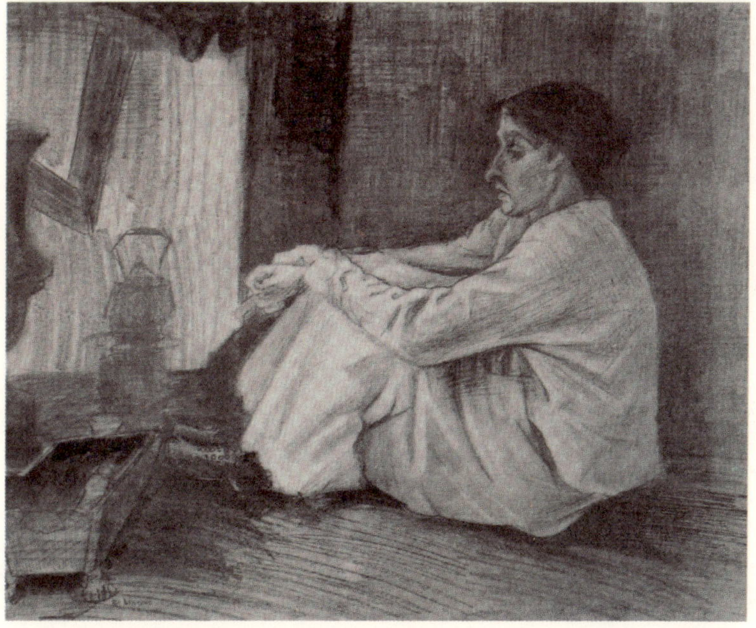

Sien with Cigar, sitting on the floor, April 1882

One sketchy work is a fine portrait of her. Vincent was used to looking at black and white prints, and understood the power of contrast. Sien sits in her white underclothes near a washing line suspended across a bare room. Included are the stove, the kettle and a cradle in an empty corner. Sien, reflective here as she smokes, has not yet given birth, but Vincent anticipates the baby's arrival with a pious sense of paternity.

The studio also became a place of invention where his models posed in imaginary scenes like tableaux. Yet reality did not escape him. Windows in the places where he lived were like lookout posts on the world. With sure handling Vincent carefully drew the outside scene – the carpenters' yard and laundry.

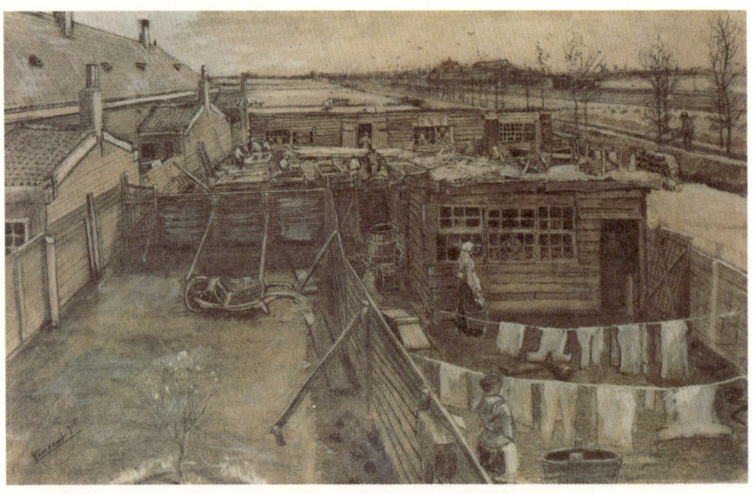

Carpenter's Workshop from the Artist's Studio, 1882

The view was difficult, with a foreground full of crowded detail and lines of fencing and sheds at right angles. Where he sat, he saw the edges of town reach to a rural area on a high horizon line. To achieve this kind of work, Vincent had a perspective frame made which he described to Theo.

"It makes it possible to compare the proportions of objects close at hand with those on a plane further away, in cases where construction according to the rules of perspective isn't feasible. Which, if you do it by eye, will always come out wrong, unless you're very experienced and skilled."

Letter from Vincent van Gogh to Theo van Gogh with sketches of Post for perspective frame

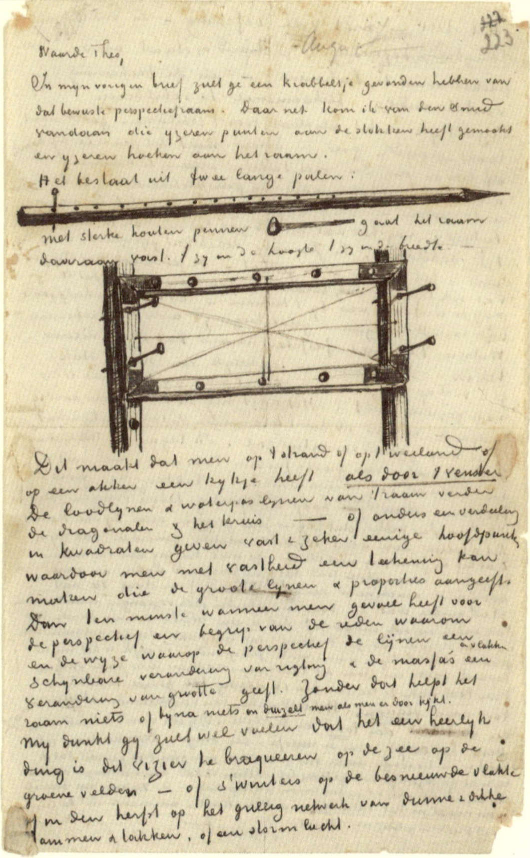

This wooden rectangle was crossed with wires to provide a pattern of threads. Each smaller section offered a guide to recreating the correct proportions and distancing of the scene in front of him. Traces of the grid lines remain on the paper of his great drawing. Much of it is heightened with white, to relieve and enhance the monotone colouring. None of the laundresses and the carpenters, a peasant wheeling a cart on a path, even animals in a far field are 'types', but they are all placed in their natural environment, hard at work.

In June 1882 Sien gave birth to a boy. Soon after he visited them, Vincent rented a bigger apartment next door and put all his energy into creating a domestic haven for the ready-made family he saw as his own. Theo, now in charge of a monthly allowance to keep Vincent's art afloat, insisted he did not marry Sien – such a marriage would prove disastrous. With his knowledge of the art market, Theo advised him to concentrate on landscape painting, preferably in colour. Vincent's new shopping list – with oil paints and brushes – was extensive, but he assured Theo he would soon be living in a real painter's studio.

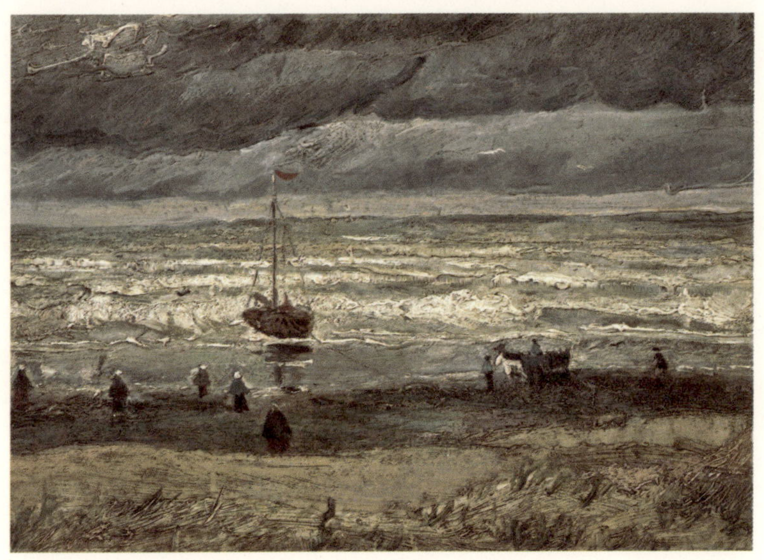

View of the Sea at Scheveningen, 1882

In August, Vincent took his bulky equipment out to the dunes of Scheveningen, a long sandy beach on the northwest edge of The Hague. Here in a raging storm, he set up his easel, his perspective frame and his paints that were all threatened by the wind. He composed a scene of the beach divided into horizontal bands with human activity along the lower line of the seashore. He laid muted tones of grey and brown on to the canvas in thick sweeps of paint where sand particles lodged.

"I find painting so appealing that I'll have to make a great effort not to paint all the time. It's rather more manly than watercolour, and has more poetry to it."

Vincent returned to work outdoors frequently, often in bad weather. His contemporaries of The Hague School, including Mauve, painted many landscape scenes and when Vincent wrote about nature, he described its colours, its changeability and his delight in capturing its many effects. The sand dunes of Scheveningen provided him with his first real experience of the difficulties and rewards of the painter's craft, and the great versatility of oils.

Still he believed he should return to draw the human figure. As the summer of 1882 ended, he haunted the street markets and bustling activity of the Geest, working on the spot or looking out for models. In this large output of work, the people he watched and drew still remained 'types' that resembled Millet's peasants or the characters in popular prints. Always moved by the plight of the poor he witnessed, by the autumn he was recording

"the sort of people of whom it's impossible to say what they do or how they live, but who evidently potter along and fret and get on with life."

In his depiction of the local lottery office, he drew hopeful people stooped by ill health and poverty. They form a large group as they enter the gaping office door that stands in the centre of the scene. Vincent's street views found a new vitality in watercolour. This enabled him to introduce colour to the scenes and soften the lines of some of his more harshly drawn sketches.

When he approached his landlord for expensive changes to be made to his studio, Vincent hoped that Sien might have an attic room for herself. The studio was also to be a place of refuge for his down-at-heel models. But as the winter of early 1883 progressed, so his

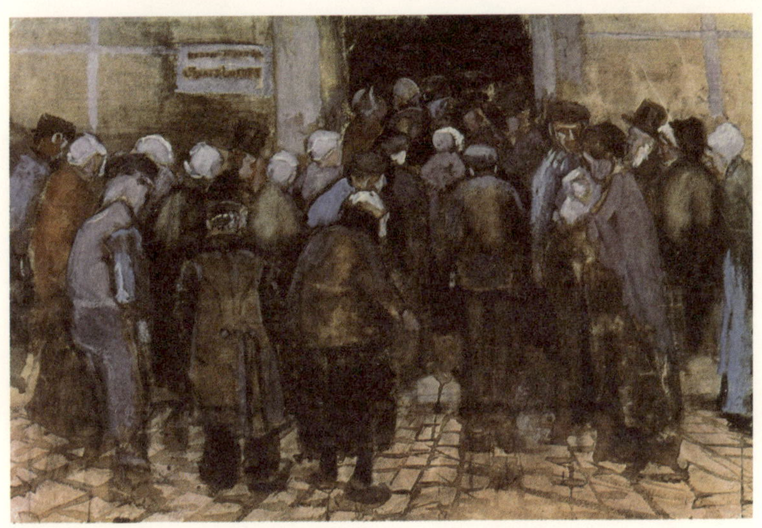

The State Lottery Office, 1883

relations with Sien deteriorated. He found his initial love for her, sprung from his compassionate nature, was **"now as prosaic as Monday morning."** Yet his affection for her baby developed as the boy grew, and Vincent feared that if they separated, she would return to prostitution.

Money was always a problem. The idea of leaving The Hague to live more cheaply in a small village began to enter his thoughts. In just under two years he had explored all the city could offer. Doggedly he had pursued his figure drawing and sold none of the results. He had also lost the company of fellow painters. Theo suggested a move to Paris or further north, which would greatly reduce the expenses he paid. Although Vincent had hoped to take Sien with him when he finally left The Hague, they agreed to go their separate ways.

"... a simple thought that seems to me right, precisely because of its simplicity, is that I should take no steps more than to live more cheaply by moving to the country, somewhere where the land has character."

....

Vincent set his mind on going to the region of **DRENTHE,** in the northeast of the Netherlands. His friend Rappard knew it and had told him about its specific mood and original kind of landscape. He also found the people there reminded him of Vincent's own work. The possibility of like-minded artists working together always attracted Vincent and he thought Drenthe might give him this opportunity. He left The Hague on a long journey, a distance of some 200km.

"I have a map of Drenthe in front of me. On it I see a large white area with no names of villages. It's crossed by the Hoogeveen waterway, which ends suddenly, and I see the words Peat moors written on the map straight across the blank area. Around that blank area a number of black dots with the names of villages, a red dot for the small town of Hoogeveen."

Hoogeveen was indeed a dot in a desolate landscape of moorland. The village was one long row of houses. The nearby terrain was like a vast swamp held together by peat.

"In the village harbour I saw really authentic peat barges and the figures of bargemen. Women wearing the local costume in the hayfield – fine. It will probably be even more beautiful deeper into the countryside, but meanwhile I'm already seeing very good things – even here."

As he walked and watched the changing light on rough homesteads, the area and the people reminded him of Barbizon scenes. The bleak heath peopled by men, women and children whose gruelling work was to load the horse-drawn barges, he saw as a picturesque, noble scene.

"... the melancholy which things in general have, is of a healthy kind, as in Millet's drawings."

The canals, at different times of day, were like mirrors of coloured light. Dark, straight horizon lines were broken by the massive heaps of peat stacks. Vincent recorded the area's bleakness with the eyes of someone enchanted.

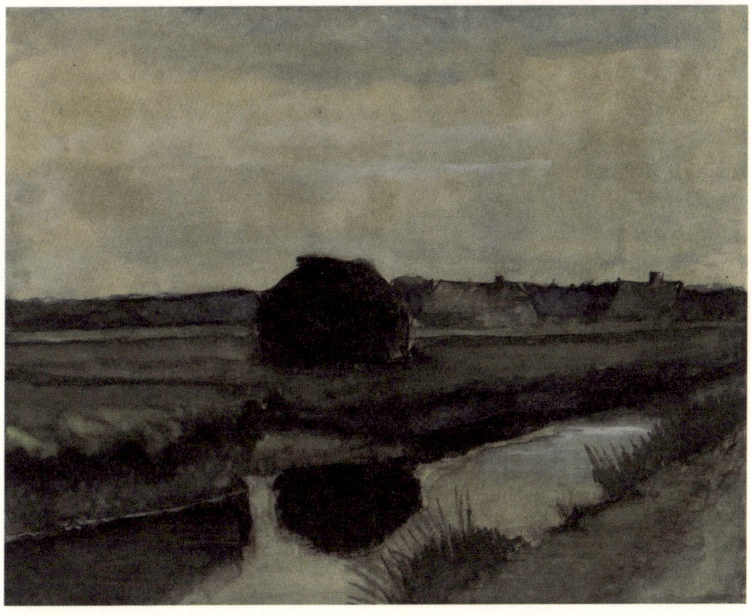

Landscape with a Stack of Peat and Farmhouses, 1883

However, it was not long before he was hurled into loneliness. He found few models to pose for him, as they thought him strange and ridiculous. Worst of all, he regretted leaving Sien and the children, and worried what had become of them. This in turn led to fears over his own uncertain existence.

After only three weeks he took a barge on a six-hour journey of 30km to Nieuw-Amsterdam, deeper inside the oppressive countryside. Still he found Barbizon in the landscape and inherent in this, great beauty. He tried to keep positive.

"I now have a reasonably large room where a stove has been placed, where there happens to be a small balcony. From which I can even see the heath with the huts. I also look out on a very curious drawbridge. Well, downstairs is an inn and a peasant kitchen with an open peat fire, very cosy in the evenings. One can think best by one of those peasant hearths with a cradle beside it."

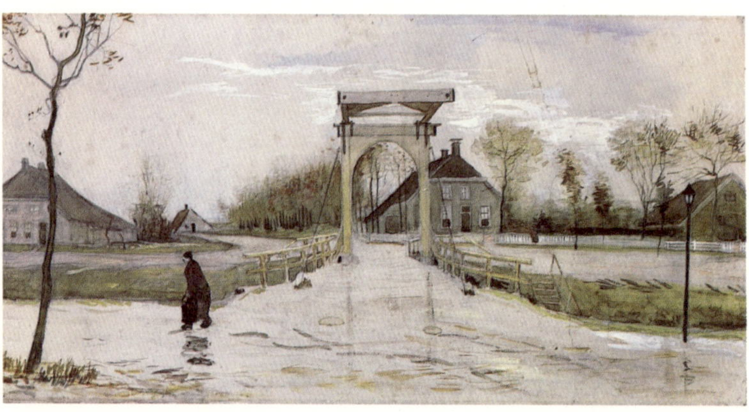

Drawbridge in Nieuw Amsterdam, 1883

Vincent was able to stave off depression by working. Looking out from yet another window at the scene ahead, he created in his watercolour painting a perfectly composed image where one single figure walks by. It referred to his past work, with its clear division of grounds and, in the central motif of the bridge, prefigured paintings to come.

One early morning Vincent took an open cart to the village of Zweeloo, a journey of three hours. He wrote an ecstatic, vivid description of the journey, the landscape and the people.

"One feels exactly as if one had been at an exhibition
of one hundred masterpieces."

His optimism changed, however, when faced with his own abject poverty. The approach of winter was about to defeat him. Theo had became unsettled at work and in his isolation Vincent began an irrational campaign inciting his brother to leave the firm – and to become his painting companion. He hoped his attack on Goupil & Cie, and the art market in general, would encourage Theo to leave. It was also a defence of his own failures. Eventually, he said that if Theo did not come, he would no longer accept his money. Theo, he claimed, was being dehumanised in Paris.

Irrational thinking was often the result of Vincent's hopes being thwarted, as well as his isolation. The idea that Theo, who had no ambitions to be an artist, would leave his secure job and join him was nonsense. The hardship of the place and Vincent's loneliness there had made him become very ill. By the end of December 1883, after only three months in Drenthe, he walked 25 kilometres across the heath in a snowstorm back to the station at Hoogeveen.

"I thought that being at home again might give me a more accurate insight into the question of what I should do."

....

He had not seen both parents for two years, though his father had visited him briefly in The Hague. Once again they had moved, this time to a parsonage in **NUENEN** in the Brabant. Within a few days of his arrival, Vincent recalled his previous exile from home. He saw himself as no better than an ugly and rough dog in his parents' eyes. His complaints were aimed towards his father, who, despite the antagonism, this time agreed to convert the laundry room at the back of the house into a studio for Vincent.

'We don't think it's a particularly suitable place, but we've had a decent stove put in there,' his father wrote to Theo. 'We had it spruced up and have even had a bed put in there ... so that it won't be unhealthy. Now we shall just make it nice and warm and dry and then it should do.'

Vincent soon explored the land nearby. A weaving industry had developed in some of the homes of Nuenen peasants. The weavers, their materials and their cottages now became his motifs that he drew and painted, often in watercolour. Weaving looms were big, heavy structures that presented Vincent with awkward views, sometimes masking the figures behind them. He persevered in his observation of this new form of manual work and spent many hours indoors, in close contact with such neighbours.

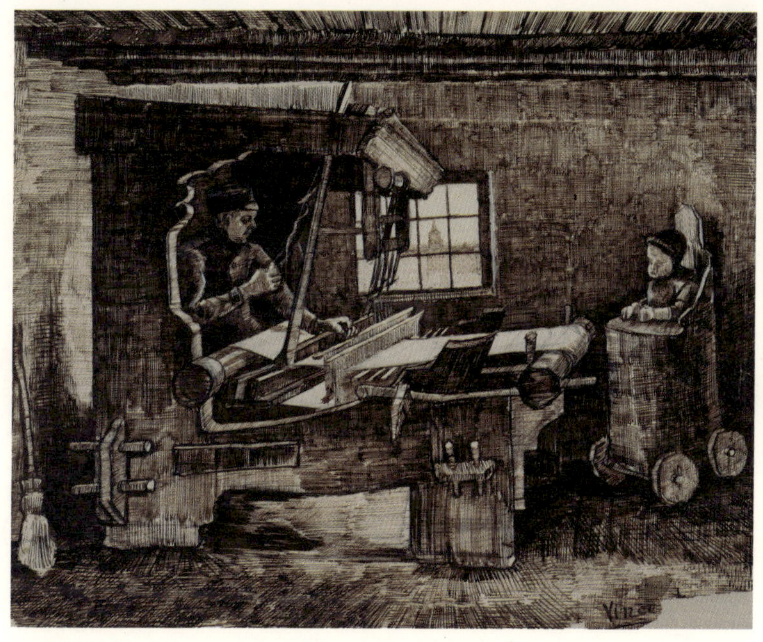

Weaver with a Baby in a High Chair, 1884

"I'm also painting a loom – of old oak gone greenish brown – with the date 1730 carved into it. Next to that loom, by a little window through which one can see a small green field, there's a high chair, and the little child sits in it, watching the weaver's shuttle fly back and forth for hours. I've tackled that affair just as it is in reality, the loom with the little weaver, the small window and that high chair in the wretched little room with the clay floor."

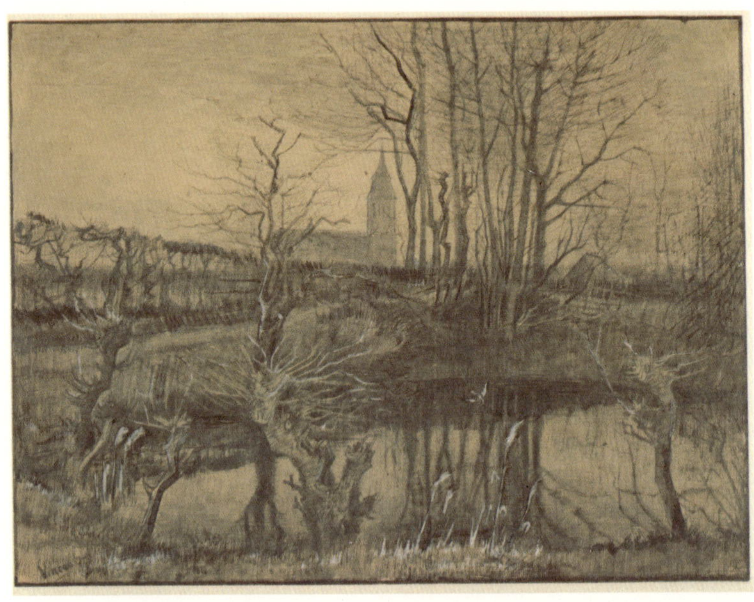

The Kingfisher, 1884

Here in Nuenen, without knowing it, he moved towards the resolution he sought in his work. Nature was a saleable subject – and in itself a source of healing.

"That absorption in the moment – that being so wholly and utterly carried away and inspired by the surrounding in which one happens to be – what can one do about it? And even if one could resist it if one wanted to, what would be the point, why shouldn't one give oneself over to that which is in front of one, as this, after all, is the surest way to create something."

In May Vincent moved his work out of his parents' home, convinced he would do better away from the parsonage. His new studio consisted of two rooms in the house of the Catholic sexton and his wife on Kerkstraat, the main street through Nuenen. He was to pay 75 guilders a year for a place that would offer him more room to pose models. To succeed in figure drawing, despite his lack of success in the subject, was still his primary ambition.

The theme of working people was now fixed in his mind despite Theo's advice against it. He explained that in Holland the Parisian art scene was virtually unknown. His own art was born of an admiration for another era and another place, as well as the black and white prints he knew from working in the art market. Theo urged him to seek brighter colours, but he chose to use dark pigment – bistre made from the soot of burnt wood and bitumen, frequently used by artists as an additive to paint.

"When I hear you talk about a lot of new names, it's not always possible for me to understand when I've seen absolutely nothing by them. And from what you said about 'Impressionism', I've grasped that it's something different from what I thought it was, but it's still not entirely clear to me what one should understand by it."

Vincent was not going to be diverted easily from his individual, self-imposed artistic course. However, in the autumn he was disturbed by events of a more personal nature. Next door to the parsonage lived a woman, Margot Begemann, who had kindly helped out in the household when his mother was unwell. She was older than Vincent and had grown deeply fond of him. Marriage between them was discussed but rejected by both sets of parents. Margot's reaction was an attempt at suicide by drinking poison. Shocked, Vincent watched out for her recovery that led, finally, to Margot moving away from Nuenen.

Tension mounted in the parsonage and Vincent's father, always the object of his obsessive attacks, wrote to Theo of their dilemma. 'We are doing our best to restore him to calm, which is the most important thing. But his outlook on life and his ways are so different to ours, that it's questionable whether living together in the same place can continue in the long run. However, we don't want a real separation and are willing to tolerate and attempt everything to the utmost, if only he could become a bit normal.'

The idea of going to Paris or Antwerp arose, where Vincent might sell his work, but the work he preferred kept him in Nuenen.

"I think it by no means unlikely that I'll stay here for the rest of my life, too. After all, I desire nothing other than to live deep in the country and to paint peasant life."

His parents wished he could take up other activities – even skating – but he set himself unreasonable goals and carried them out with a feverish activity that helped to mask his personal grievances. In every way he had drifted from the life his family lived and hoped he would emulate. The studio at the sexton's house in Nuenen, although not far from them, was now his refuge. Here, during the winter of early 1885, he began a new series devoted to local peasants.

"I'm working with almighty pleasure these days for I would much rather paint figures than anything else. Then – the heads of these women here with the white caps – it's difficult – but it's so eternally beautiful. It's precisely the chiaroscuro – the white and the part of the face in shadow that has such a fine tone."

Vincent found these people quieter than the suffering miners he had known, with no impulse to raise their voices in protest, despite their poverty. They allowed him into their homes where he made sketches of them and, in particular, their heads. When the weather permitted, he returned to the landscape or the parsonage garden.

In March 1885, quite unexpectedly, Vincent's father died of a stroke. Life in the parsonage changed forever. The resentment that Vincent had felt towards his father was held against him, particularly by his sister Anna. It did not take him long to move right out of home to sleep at the studio where he worked.

Vincent's father was buried at the church seen at the end of the parsonage garden. The building was in a precarious state, having collapsed a century earlier, and was now due for demolition – already its spire had gone. Vincent had often painted it – it stood as a striking, bold motif against the flat land. He decided to record it once more before its complete disappearance and gave it a distinctive character.

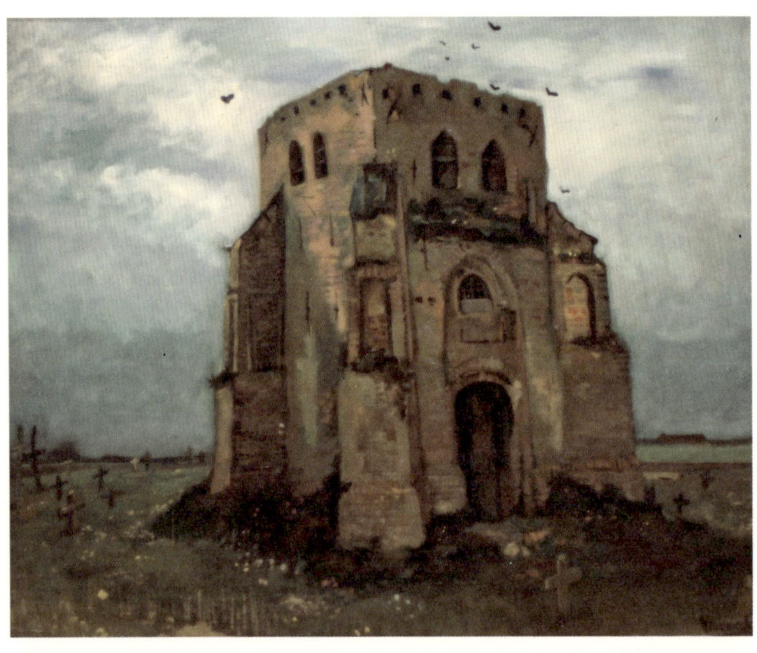

The Old Church Tower at Nuenen
('The Peasants' Churchyard), 1885

"I wanted to say how this ruin shows that for centuries the peasants have been laid to rest there in the very fields that they grubbed up in life – I wanted to say how perfectly simply death and burial happen, coolly as the falling of an autumn leaf – no more than a bit of earth turned over – a little wooden cross. The fields around – where the grass of the churchyard ends, beyond the little wall, they make a last fine line against the horizon – like the horizon of a sea. And now this ruin says to me how a faith and religion mouldered away, although it was solidly founded – how, though, the life and death of the peasants is and will always be the same, springing up and withering regularly like the grass and the flowers that grow there in that churchyard."

Now he was using oils to move beyond studies and to define the peasants' real world. Just as he had chosen the tumbled old tower as the subject for an oil painting, so he found a suitably strong motif in a rustic cottage. In both works he recorded familiar places that evoked the lives and deaths of the peasants. The deteriorated and cramped house – more like a hovel – stood stark beneath a rose-tinged sky. The old tower was lit by the evening sun. By bringing the light of rural Barbizon to the Brabant, Vincent ennobled his ruins.

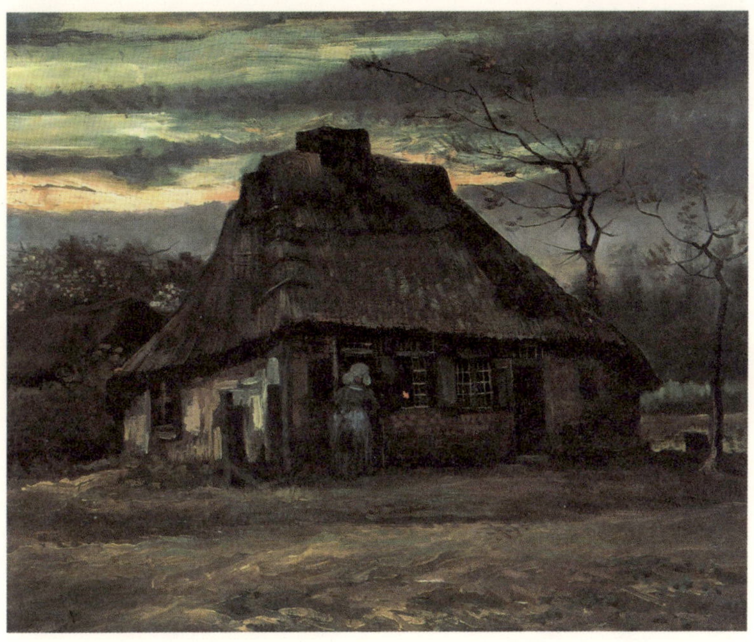

Thatched Cottage at Dusk, 1885

From his close knowledge of the peasants' lives, Vincent developed ideas for a large painting. On this he worked with countless studies of the people he knew, their heads, their hands and their traditional clothes. He felt sure it would be a significant work. The canvas shows a small group of men, women and a child gathered around a table to eat their meagre evening meal. Light falls from a single oil lamp above the table. The dark tones emphasise their poverty. He called the painting *The Potato Eaters*.

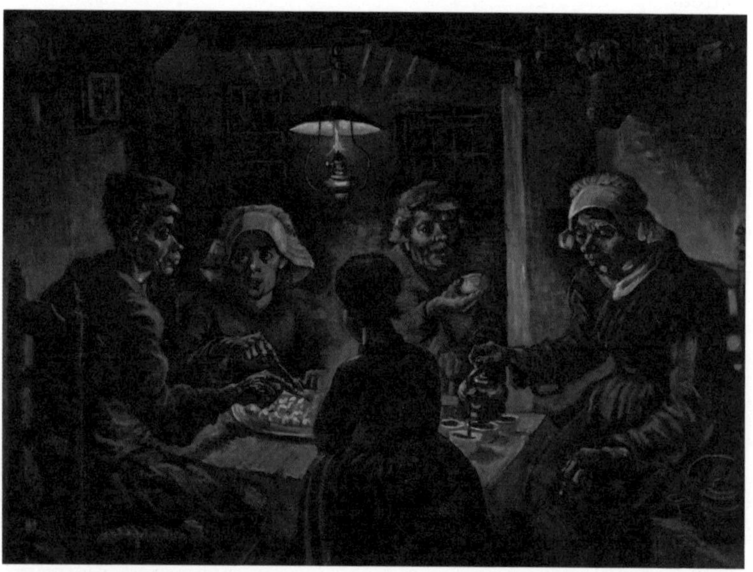

The Potato Eaters, 1885

"It's not for nothing that I've spent so many evenings sitting pondering by the fire with the miners and the peat-cutters and the weavers and peasants here – unless I had no time to think – because of the work. I've become so absorbed in peasant life by continually seeing it at all hours of the day that I really hardly ever think of anything else."

Vincent felt the painting was the best thing he had ever done. In early May he sent it to Theo in Paris, hoping it would be well received. Theo showed *The Potato Eaters* to people in his circle, but knowing he had to tread softly with his brother, he explained he might have difficulty selling it. Vincent had a lithograph impression made locally which he sent to Rappard. Unexpectedly, this friend whose criticism he always respected, was shocked. 'Such a work isn't intended seriously....' he claimed in a letter full of strong complaints. Rappard's views caused a serious rift in their friendship.

Life in Nuenen became more strained when he was implicated in the pregnancy of one of his models. Gordina de Groot was the woman with the striking, open face that featured boldly in his painting. Fingers were pointed at Vincent, the wayward, ragged artist who lived away from home and mixed with such people of the lower classes. The local priesthood joined in many accusations, but Vincent hoped only to stay on good terms with the peasants. For him they were part of old, Brabant stock – and the centre of his world.

A brief respite from tensions at home came in the autumn when he spent a few days away. The new Rijksmuseum had recently opened in Amsterdam and he took the opportunity of seeing its fine collection of Dutch art – and real paintings, not their black and white reproductions as prints. The experience opened his eyes.

"What particularly struck me when I saw the old Dutch paintings again is that they were usually painted quickly. That these great masters like Hals, Rembrandt, Ruisdael – so many others – as far as possible just put it straight down – and didn't come back to it very much."

Vincent, too, was an artist now. He looked closely at the brushstrokes and saw the way in which colours had been laid on countless canvases. He guessed how these had been mixed, and wrote at length to Theo with long lists of artists' names, their subjects and their styles. Their correspondence turned to the scientific aspects of colour that his Parisian contemporaries were examining at the time.

"... if you find some book or other on colour questions, that is good, do be sure to send it to me, for I too know far from everything about it, and go on searching every day."

Vincent's painting of the parsonage was a form of memento of the life his family had lived and that was now in the past. Like his other recordings of houses, it is seen from across the road, opposite its façade. To the right is the neighbouring barn. The tall windows have their curtains neatly tied. A warm autumn light falls throughout the golden scene, complemented by the brilliant blue of the sky. Two women talk at the front gate.

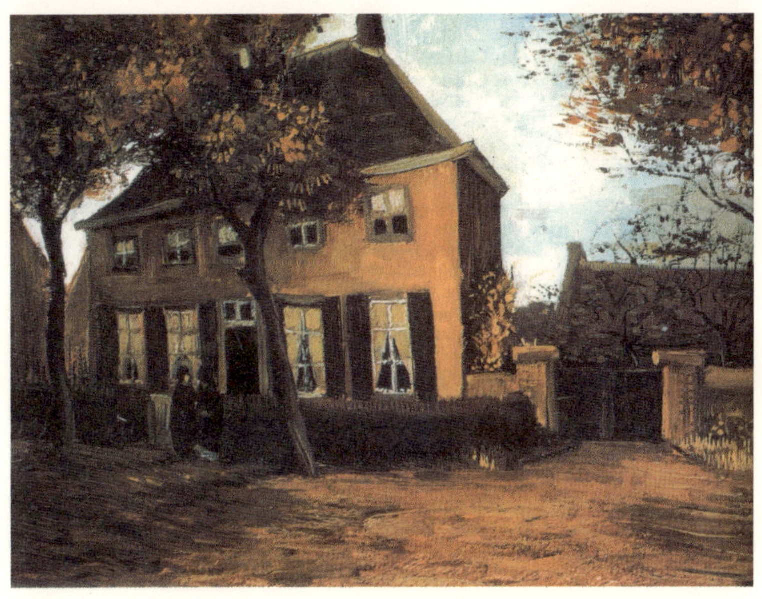

The Vicarage at Neunen, 1885

With plans underway for his mother to leave Nuenen, Vincent also considered another move. His social identity in the village had suffered greatly. He had befriended peasants and had accompanied their young in search of birds' nests. His reputation was further blackened from his relationships with two very different women. He may have been the deceased vicar's son, but his unconventional ways were unwelcome.

It was time to promote the work he had achieved with a serious sales campaign in a thriving town. Vincent set his mind on Antwerp.

"I have to choose between a studio without work here, and work without a studio there. I took the latter. And with pleasure that's actually so great that it feels to me like a return from exile. After all, I've been out of the world of painting altogether for a long time."

When he set off for Belgium from Nuenen, Vincent at the age of thirty-two left home for the last time.

"I've rented a little room, rue des Images, No. 194, above a paint merchant, for 25 francs a month."

....

In his little room in **ANTWERP,** Vincent soon hung up pictures that would make the rented space feel more welcoming. Among these were Japanese prints that he found 'very diverting'.

His object now was to comb the print shops with a view to selling his figure drawings, and within a short time he wandered about the city, making new discoveries. The dockland, with its thriving, bustling trade, was chaotic, noisy and entertaining.

"I've already walked in all directions around these docks and wharves several times. It's a strange contrast, particularly when one comes from the sand and the heath and the tranquillity of a country village and hasn't been in anything but quiet surroundings for a long time. It's an incomprehensible confusion."

He found no buyers for his work. Disheartened, he had no choice but to carry on. Once again, his chosen subject was figures, although

there were no peasants in Antwerp. The great port teemed with
dockers, sailors and prostitutes.

*"My thoughts are full of Rembrandt and Hals at the moment, not because
I see many paintings by them but because I see so many types among the
people here who remind me of that age. I still often go to the dance halls to
see these women's heads and sailors' or soldiers' heads."*

He did not draw or paint with any more accuracy than when he had
depicted the characterful heads of peasants in his homeland. He
befriended a girl working in the Scala music hall, painted her portrait
and soon found the paid company of women a welcome diversion.
A novel idea was that he should paint nudes, and he became familiar
with the work of Rubens, who had died in Antwerp and was well
represented there. Although he likened Rubens' female saints to
a pretty whore, he admired his colouring and painterly technique.

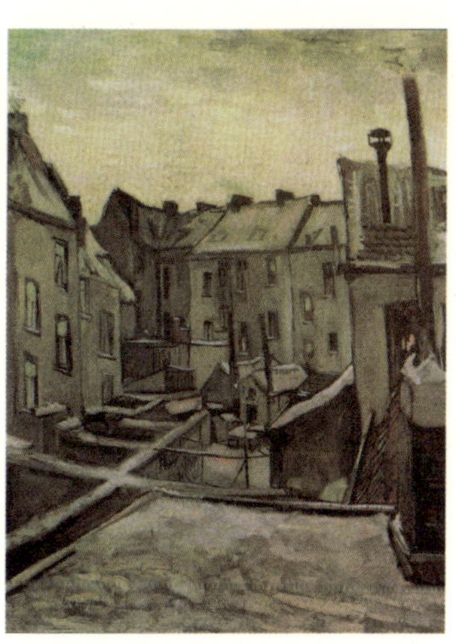

*Houses seen in Antwerp
in the snow from the
back, 1885–6*

From his window he painted the backs of houses he looked out upon.
Windows, like his perspective frame, provided the scope for these
views and he always found the immediate scenes worth recording –
as if they provided documents of where he lived. However, as a studio
his little room was limited. In order to sell, he thought of painting
notable city landmarks. One large and famous building was the
medieval fortress, Het Steen, that rose in the centre of the old town.

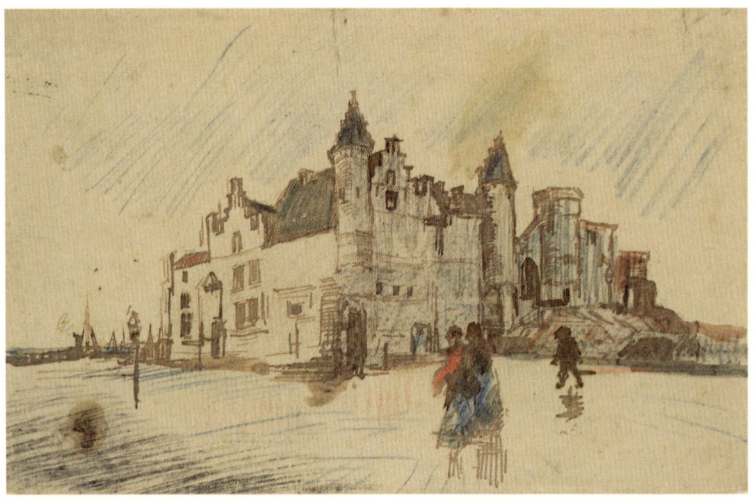

View of Het Steen, 1885

As with the smaller buildings he had drawn or painted before,
Vincent placed the great monument centre stage. For this he had to
stand some distance away from it. Broad walls and tall towers form
a voluminous bulk on the page. In the wide, empty foreground he
animated the scene with figures, some daubed with colour. The whole
image is drawn with a brisk, sure hand.

Although he worked hard to create saleable works and to improve his
drawing technique, Vincent knew he still needed substantial training.
In mid-January 1886, he enrolled for classes at the Royal Academy in
Antwerp, hopeful he would find nude models there, as well as the
company of other painters. His odd clothes and his furious manner of
painting caused a sensation. More significantly, he was only allowed
to study from plaster casts – his objection to this had caused the
rift with his cousin Mauve. Alternative classes in the evening, set up
by Academy students, did include nude models and, for the sake of
learning, he liked to compare the real thing with the casts.

After only a month or two, things were not turning out as he had
hoped. Money was the usual problem – and paying prostitutes
with the portraits he had done of them was not going to improve
his finances or his art. Although he claimed he gained much from
his teachers, he was often at odds with them. He made no sound
friendships and soon the degenerating state of his health could not
be overlooked.

Should he move to Paris, and Theo? He believed they could set up a
studio together where similarly struggling artists could meet. During
the early weeks of 1886 the idea was bandied about between them
as Vincent found it the perfect plan, then retreated and claimed the

country was really his place. Theo's replies became less frequent so, characteristically, Vincent began an onslaught of persuasion.

"It seems to me that such an arrangement or something similar would be perfectly satisfactory for the first year. What I'm not sure about is whether we'll get on personally, although I don't despair of it – but it'll be much more agreeable for you to come home to a workplace than to an ordinary room, which always has something gloomy about it. And it's that gloom that's our worst enemy. When the doctor tells me that I have to take better care of myself, physically – well, who knows whether such a measure mightn't do you good too."

Theo explained there could be no such move until his rent was paid up at the end of June. Alternatively, Vincent could go back to Nuenen, continue working there and help their mother with her move from the parsonage.

"Today – Sunday – it was almost a spring day – this morning I went for a long walk on my own, all through the city, in the park, along the boulevard. It was such weather that in the countryside one would probably have heard the lark for the first time. And in short there was something of a resurrection in the atmosphere."

Antwerp still held great appeal for Vincent the observer and lover of nature, but he was hardly able to survive there. None of his work, including the city views, was sold. He was becoming very ill, was hospitalised and underwent considerable dental treatment. It was winter. With no warning, he abandoned the city, intent on joining his brother in Paris.

When he arrived, Vincent left Theo a note.

"Don't be cross with me that I've come all of a sudden. I've thought about it so much and I think we'll save time this way. Will be at the Louvre from midday.... We'll sort things out, you'll see. So get there as soon as possible...."

Theo's apartment in rue Laval, a small street in the north of the city, had little space for the two men as well as Vincent's working materials. However, in order to adapt to a new life with his brother – and to please him – Vincent began by smartening up his appearance. The plan initially was that he should study further, this time taking the conventional way of all artists who, embarking on their careers, learned from a respected master. Fernand Cormon (1845–1924), a favourite of the Salon, held his open studio not far from the apartment and Vincent believed a three-year period under his guidance would set him on the right road.

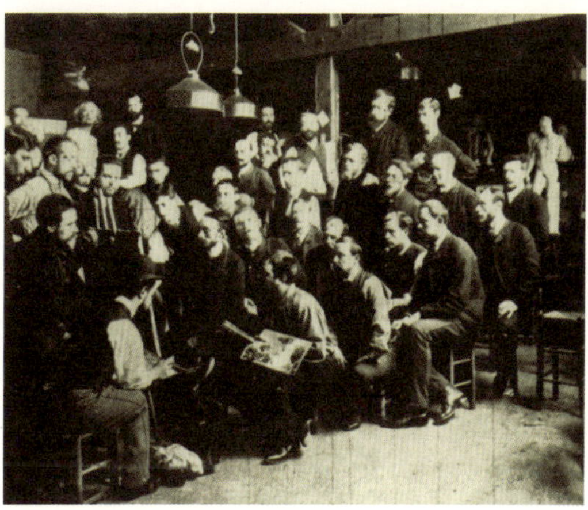

In Cormon's Atelier

Here, although nudes occasionally posed, the main task was to draw from plaster casts. Cormon examined his students' drawing techniques and found little merit in Vincent's work. The speed with which he painted also caused alarm. For a while Vincent persevered with this formal training until he left in the summer – during which time his work completely changed direction.

The brothers found a new self-contained apartment with enough rooms to provide Vincent with a studio. The rue Lepic was the main road leading up to Montmartre where the huge church, Sacre Coeur, was still being built. This semi-rural hill attracted sightseers away from the city to the open air where a few old windmills survived.

In May, for one month, the eighth and final exhibition of works by the Impressionists took place. Vincent felt no great liking for their work. One young artist – Georges Seurat (1859–91) – caused a great stir at the exhibition.

Seurat had examined many scientific theories on how colour is perceived. He developed a style of painting that acknowledged this, and instead of mixing colours on the palette, he applied them pure, in tiny dots. When standing away from the canvas, the eye did the mixing. This style became known as 'Pointillism'. Colours could also change in intensity, according to their proximity to other colours. The colour wheel, established by scientists and used by artists, revealed which colours lay opposite each other as complementary colours (also known as 'complementaries).

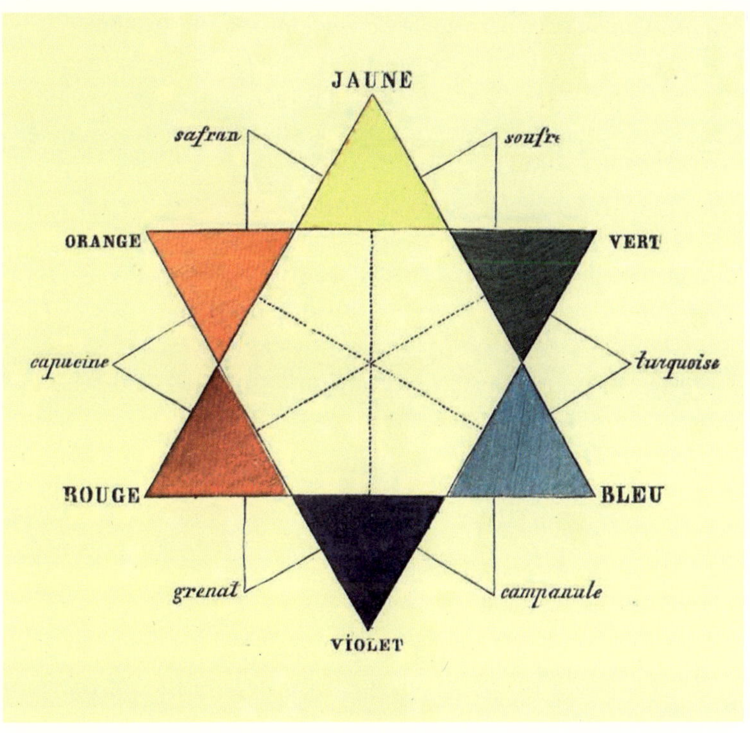

Charles Blanc's colour wheel

The painter Eugène Delacroix (1798–1863), whom Vincent admired, had also examined and put to use these theories. The more he studied them himself, the more Vincent was liberated from his previous colour schemes. With flowers in abundance in the warmer weather, he created his own colour experiments.

"I have lacked money for paying models, else I had entirely given myself up to figure painting but I have made a series of colour studies in painting simply flowers, red poppies, blue corn flowers and myosotys. White and rose roses, yellow chrysanthemums – seeking oppositions of blue with orange, red and green, yellow and violet, seeking THE BROKEN AND NEUTRAL TONES to harmonise brutal extremes. Trying to render intense COLOUR and not a grey harmony."

Another artist whom both brothers admired, and who Vincent came to emulate, was Adolphe Monticelli (1824–86). His vases of flowers and rural scenes were achieved with richly coloured, thick daubs of paint that gave his canvases a rough, textured surface. Theo hoped to sell his work at the gallery.

Away from the city side of Montmartre, Vincent liked to work outdoors, on the open, rural hilltop. It was not far to walk from the apartment and offered him a welcome change from the city's concrete. Some of the old windmills there had been adapted into public places of entertainment. Vincent was drawn to these landmarks, so reminiscent of his homeland, and made many paintings from different angles of their bold structure that stood as silhouettes against the sky. Ten years earlier, Pierre-Auguste Renoir (1841–1919) had painted a lively ball at the Moulin de la Galette.

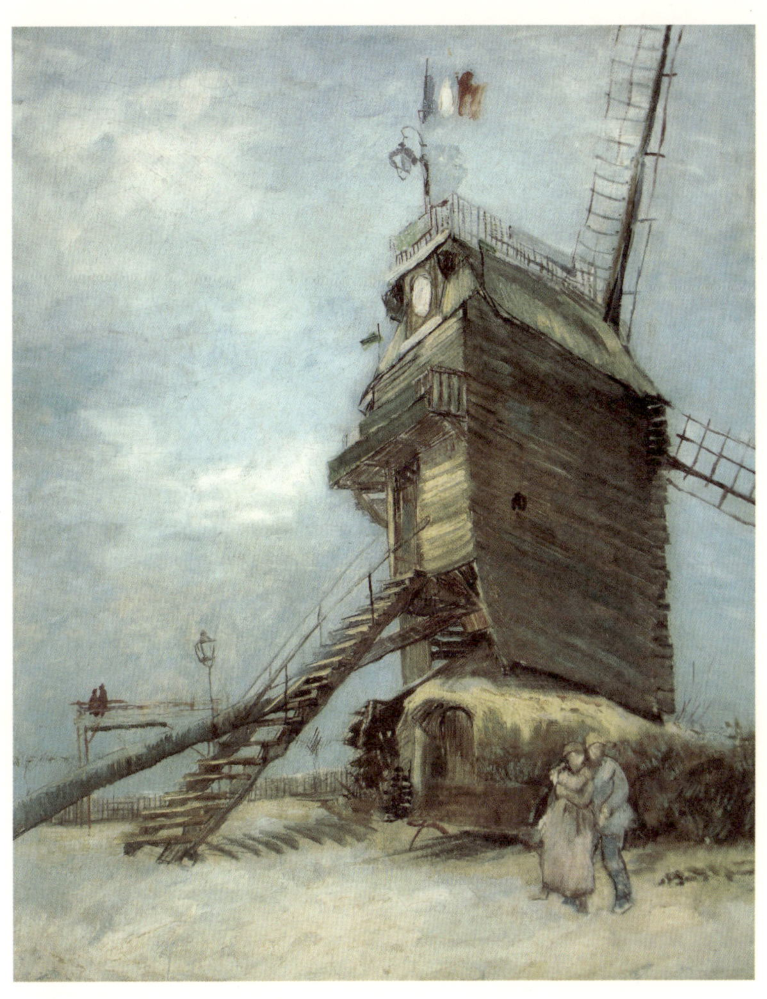

Le Moulin de la Galette, 1886

Vincent made many paintings of the site and of some of the buildings
he found there. The Blute-Fin windmill stands motionless as it looms
above the ground. Its wooden walls, ramp and outstretched sails,
together with a stack of wheat, recall its working life. Vincent placed
people in the foreground – this time a couple. The bearded man in
rough working clothes, so like a self-portrait, takes a gentle stroll
with his girl.

The two brothers had not lived together for any length of time
since they were children. As adults they shared the intrigues of their
numerous love affairs. In letters they had spoken only guardedly of
the health hazards of venereal diseases, so prevalent among the
sexually active. Theo, through his work, mixed easily in sophisticated
circles, whereas Vincent remained distinctly bohemian. Domestic
arrangements in the apartment, that Vincent kept with no regard for
order, threatened a peaceful life when it came to others visiting. In
the summer of 1886, after working for over thirteen years in the same
company, Theo thought of setting up independently as a dealer with
a Dutch friend, Andries Bonger (1861–1936). When he returned briefly
to the Netherlands to look for financial support, Andries stayed with
Vincent in the apartment to keep him company.

As his output of paintings grew, Vincent's need to sell them became
imperative. He was now meeting other artists in the same situation
as himself. One of Cormon's students was an amusing, handicapped
aristocrat, Count Henri Marie Raymond de Toulouse-Lautrec (1864–
1901). Another was a very young and original artist, Émile Bernard
(1868–1941). They agreed their formal training was out of step with
their ideals. How could they become recognised?

An unusual outlet for exhibiting was the paint-shop of Père Tanguy (1825–94), nearby in Montmartre. His jolly nature attracted artists who bought his supplies and were grateful to have their work hung on his shop's walls. Another idea was to show in cafés, and Vincent approached the Café du Tambourin, a restaurant and cabaret nearby that was run by an Italian, Agostina Segatori (1841–1910). The café tabletops and stools were carved and painted to resemble tambourines. Another attraction was Agostina herself – as a model she had posed for Corot and Manet. Vincent and she began a close relationship.

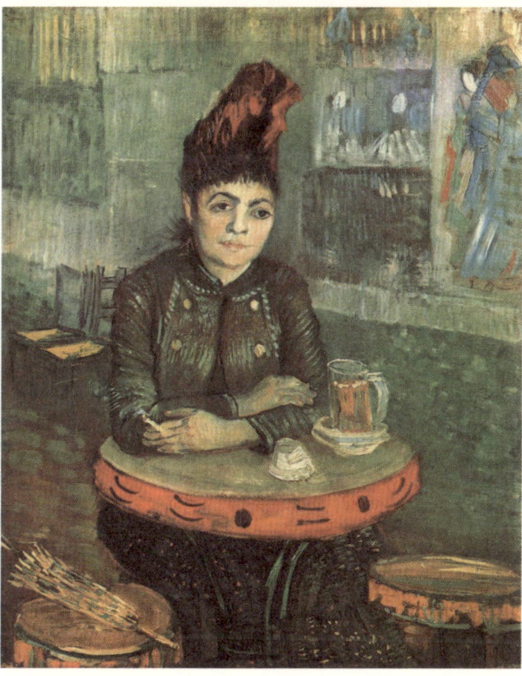

In the Café: Agostina Segatori in Le Tambourin, 1887–8

Apart from providing artists with exhibition space, these alternative galleries also displayed work that artists admired, such as Japanese prints. They are seen in the portraits that Vincent made of both Père Tanguy and Agostina. At the time, Paris was fascinated by all things Japanese. Trade with Japan had been closed for 200 years until the mid-century. After this, artworks such as woodblock prints began to appear on the market and in various shops. Their popularity grew. The prints revealed a different way of representing the world, so unlike European traditions. Flat areas of colour produced from the printing process eliminated light and shade. Outline defined form and suggested perspective. This simplified style that some artists now adopted was in complete opposition to the painstaking application of dots that had attracted others to Pointillism.

Vincent's experiments with colour, that he called 'gymnastics', now contributed to a maturing individual style. In early 1887 he met the painter Paul Signac (1863–1935) who practised the Pointillist technique that Vincent began to adopt. The view he painted from his window in the apartment (now a habit, wherever he lived) shows how it suited his experiments. The brushstrokes are applied in dots of pure colour. Pairs of colours complement each other – the red shutters framing green interiors, blue alongside yellow tones. The buildings are outlined, with no reference to shade, but suffused with an opaque city light.

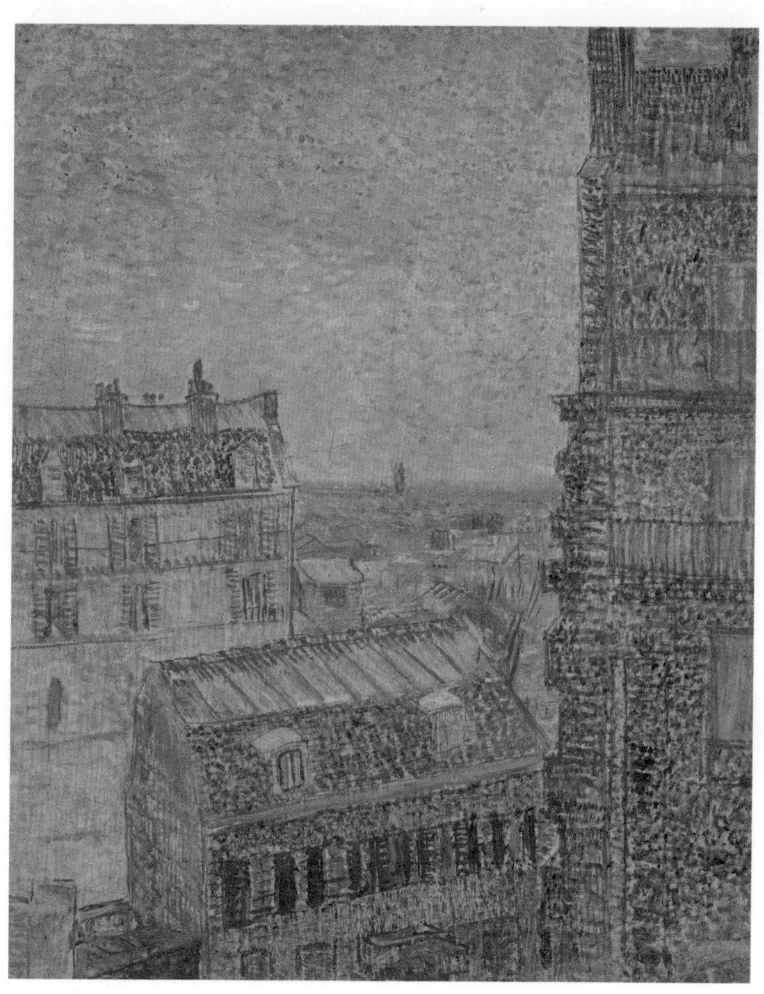

View From Theo's Apartment, 1887

In the spring, Vincent visited popular haunts on the Seine that had been favourites of the Impressionists. On public holidays, suburbs out of town became crowded with strolling Parisians. Views of the river with its dappled surface were painted by Alfred Sisley (1839–99), Renoir and Claude Monet (1840–1926), among others. Vincent frequently worked in the semi-industrial suburb, Asnières, a manageable walk from the apartment to the northwest of the city. He painted a lone fisherman who waits patiently for his catch beneath a blaze of contrasting blue, yellow and green. The brushstrokes are clearly visible, applied briskly in directional moves over each of the painting's motifs. Sunlight fills the scene. Like Signac, who sometimes accompanied him, Vincent carried the paint strokes over the frame to create further contrasted colouring.

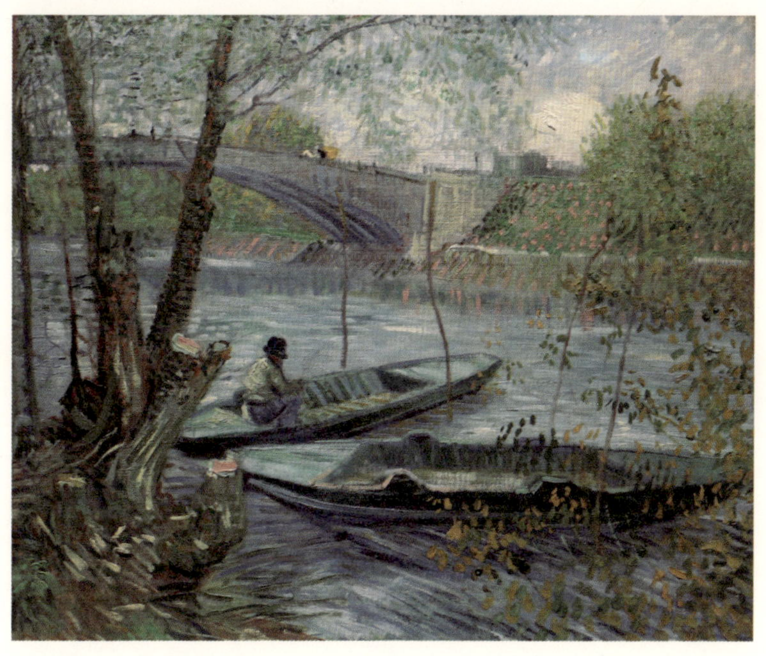

Fishing in Spring, the Pont de Clichy, 1887

Vincent often returned to Asnières in the summer to produce paintings that burst with sunshine and colour. Although he found no peasants toiling in fields, he discovered views that reached far into the distance. His depiction of factories repeats a well-tried composition that he had chosen while in the north. Horizontal bands divide the canvas into three areas, with the central line occupied by buildings and chimneys. Smoke and a cloudy sky do not throw shade on the bright red rooftops. Red, blue and green all have a place on the canvas, with yellow dominant in the foreground.

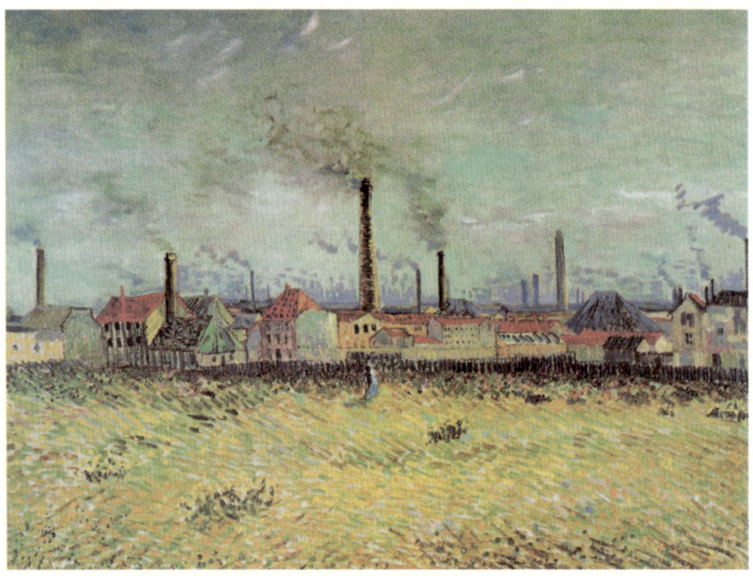

Factories at Asnières, seen from the Quay de Clichy, 1887

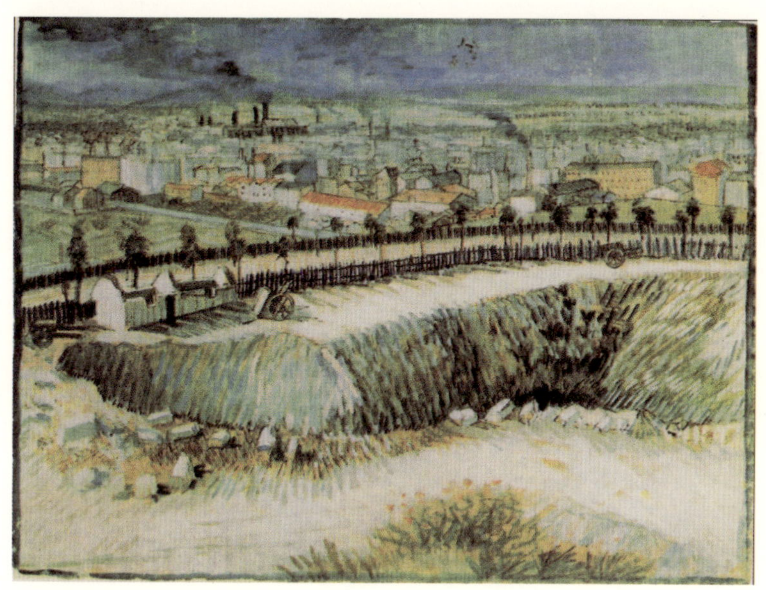

Outskirts of Paris, near Montmartre, 1887

Similarly, on a day when bad weather threatened, he chose a wide view of the distant urban landscape seen from Montmartre. Factories spew out smoke above a meticulously drawn fence that slices the composition in half. Carts have been left near a gaping quarry that dominates the open, empty foreground.

Although he adopted the methods of vanguard painters and Theo's care allowed him the freedom to work, Vincent became unsettled and quarrelsome.

"I'm going to retreat somewhere in the south so as not to see so many painters who repel me as men."

By the autumn the brothers had both shared disappointments. Theo's mission to propose to Andries Bonger's sister, Johanna (1862–1925), had ended in her refusal, as she did not know him well enough. Vincent's relations with Agostina at the Café du Tambourin had also disintegrated. Despite the great leaps he was making in his colourful work, Vincent had sold nothing. Occasionally artists exchanged work, though this was hardly profitable. The idea of going away from Paris – south – became more and more attractive to Vincent.

"My own fortunes dictate above all that I'm making rapid progress in growing up into a little old man, you know, with wrinkles, with a bristly beard, with a number of false teeth, etc. But what does that matter? I have a dirty and difficult occupation, painting…. If I didn't have Theo it wouldn't be possible for me to do justice to my work, but because I have him as a friend I believe that I'll make more progress and that things will run their course. It's my plan to go to the south for a while, as soon as I can, where there's even more colour and even more sun."

Life in the apartment on rue Lepic was not entirely peaceful, but at Theo's workplace, things changed for the better. The company, still known by some as Goupil's, had reorganised its management. With younger partners in charge, old stock was sold off to make room for more modern art. Theo was appointed to look out for marginal work and at the Montmartre gallery a specific space – a mezzanine – was given over to this art.

With a greater workload dealing with hopeful artists, Theo enlisted his brother's help. Now they worked together, a longstanding dream of Vincent's. He met up with Toulouse-Lautrec and Bernard, and at last envisaged the possibility of becoming a group of like-minded souls. To this end, Vincent planned a special exhibition of their work.

By November the location was chosen – a big, working-class restaurant nearby that had tall, empty walls. Vincent often ate there – he had once used a menu to sketch a city scene. The food was good and cheap.

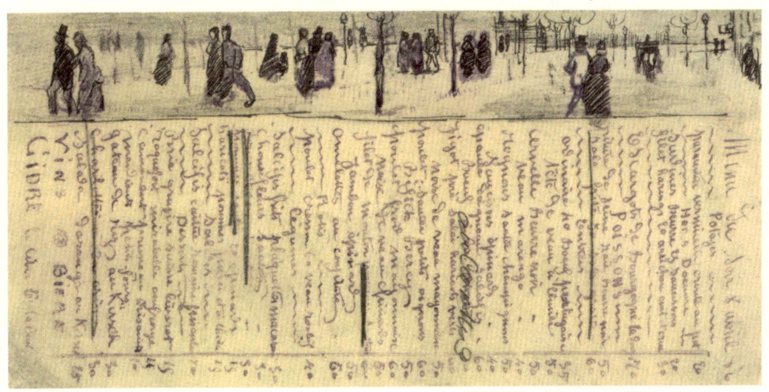

Restaurant Menu, 1886

The restaurant's owner was willing to hang paintings by Vincent and four others, and they soon searched for a name. The Impressionists were known as painters of the Grand Boulevard, since many of their works were of the wide, long avenues recently created throughout central Paris. Vincent liked the idea of his lesser-known group being named as the Petit Boulevard painters. He hoped this identity and their striking work would bring them some success. Bernard later described the exhibition's failure: 'Unfortunately, this socialist exhibition of our inflammatory canvases came to a rather sorry end.'

At the time Bernard had rejected Pointillism in favour of the lessons of Japanese woodcuts to which he hoped to open his friends' eyes. Vincent, in response, made an oil copy of a print by Hiroshige (1797–1858). Such Japanese views, with a far horizon line and flat, bright colours were suited to his own vision of landscapes.

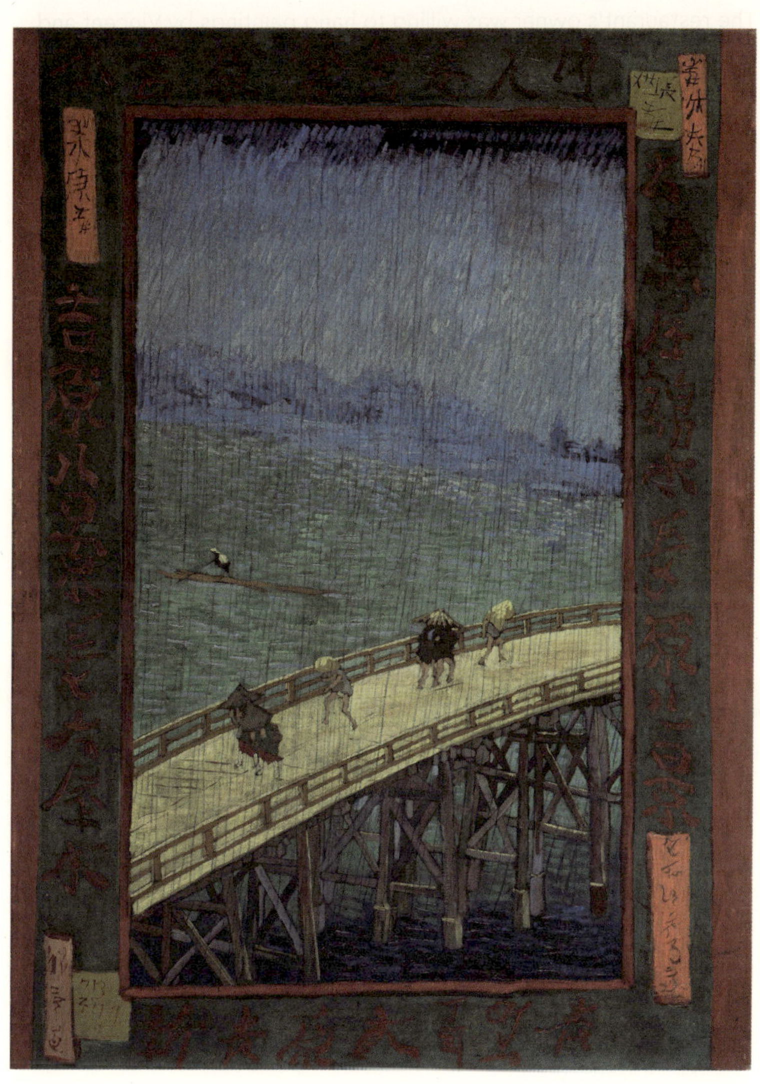

The Bridge in the Rain (after Hiroshige), 1887

Another artist who was aware of the power of Japanese art and had
visited the restaurant exhibition was Paul Gauguin (1848–1903). To gain
some attention, he aligned himself with the Impressionists, who were
now a familiar name, although his work was unlike theirs. Recently he
had returned from Martinique with paintings of a mysterious, exotic
location. Like Vincent, he sought every means to become known in
Paris and was glad to have met Theo, a potential buyer of his work.

Theo already owned five works by Monticelli, the painter from
Marseille whom both brothers admired. With new interest generated
in his work since his death, Theo hoped now to promote him. More
paintings by Monticelli were likely to still be in Provence.

Was this why Vincent left Paris – to find more Monticellis? Was it to
see the light and feel the warmth of the southern sun during the cold
winter? Was life with Theo in the city apartment, after two years,
becoming too difficult?

On 19 February 1888 Vincent left Paris by train, headed for the south.
Some days later Theo wrote about his absence to their sister Wil:

'The new school of painters tries above all to get light and sun into
paintings, and you can well understand that the grey days lately have
supplied little material for subjects. Moreover, the cold was making
him ill. The years of so much worry and adversity haven't made him
any stronger, and he felt a definite need for rather milder air. A day
and a night's travel and one is there, so the temptation was great
and he accordingly decided swiftly to go there. I believe that it
will definitely do him good, both physically and for his work. When
he came here two years ago I never thought that we'd become so

attached to each other, for there's definitely an emptiness now that I'm alone in the apartment again.'

....

When Vincent stepped off the train in **ARLES,** he already knew much about Provence. Here Monticelli had worked alongside Paul Cézanne (1839–1906), who was now living permanently in Aix. Vincent knew books by Alphonse Daudet (1840–97), the native writer of Provence. And the women of Arles, the Arlésiennes, were legendary beauties. But Arles was unlike any town Vincent had come across before.

Its history went back to classical times. Provincia, the land in Gaul conquered by the Romans, contained many fine towns and 'Arelate' was the favourite of the Emperor Constantine. At the time when Vincent arrived, its streets held many reminders of that era in substantial ruins – the Roman baths, theatre, amphitheatre and necropolis. During the Middle Ages, Arles was a major stop on the pilgrim route to Santiago de Compostela. Up until the railway's arrival, the river Rhone had provided transport and served trade throughout an extensive area. The Mediterranean was only 30 kilometres away. Provence was known for its warm climate, but when Vincent arrived Arles was suffering a brutal winter. Vincent quickly found a place to stay in the small Hotel-Restaurant Carrel in the centre of the town. Towards the end of his long journey he was struck by the landscape he had seen from the train.

"Before reaching Tarascon I noticed some magnificent scenery – huge yellow rocks, oddly jumbled together, with the most imposing shapes. In the small valleys between these rocks there were rows of little round trees with

It did not take Vincent long to walk out of the town to discover this
land. An early painting shows snow-covered fields. He had done
darker wintery scenes in the north where striving peasants worked.
Here the wide foreground is dominated by signs of rural activity, but
no people. The Arles skyline with its identifiable monuments lies on a
high horizon. The scene is dominated by a chill, winter light, reflected
from the sky onto carefully chosen complementary colours.

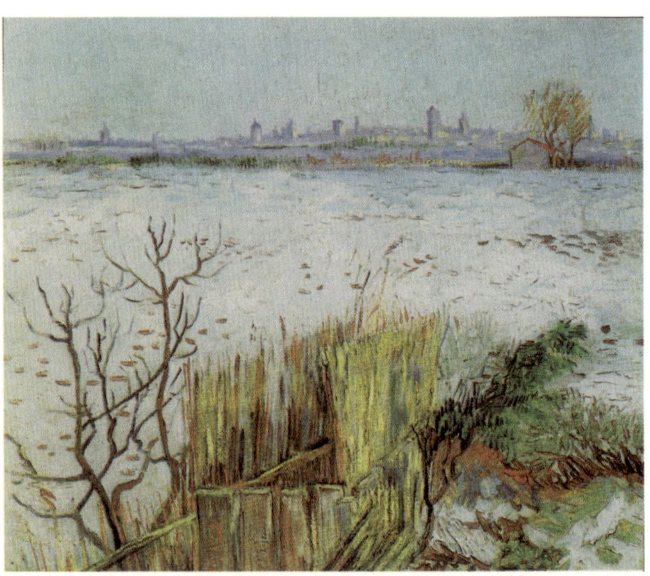

Landscape in snow with Arles in the Background, 1888

Vincent turned his back on the town of narrow streets, ruins and strangers. People spoke in a dialect he did not understand. Once warmer weather returned, fruit trees burst into blossom. He found motifs that reminded him of Japanese prints. He hoped a tree series might prove saleable and urged Theo to contact Tersteeg, their previous employer in The Hague, about this idea.

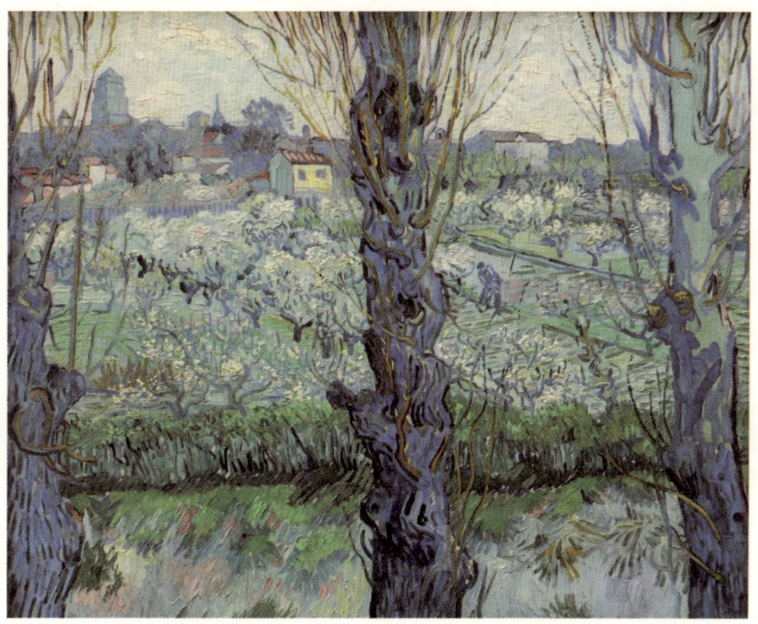

Orchard in blossom with Arles in the Background, 1888

"This morning I worked on an orchard of plum trees in blossom – suddenly a tremendous wind began to blow, an effect I'd only ever seen here – and came back again at intervals. In the intervals, sunshine that made all the little white flowers sparkle. It was beautiful! But as for the execution of what we do out of doors like this, what will they say?"

As he walked on the outskirts of town, in several directions, he also found reminders of his homeland. To the south a bridge named after the bridge-keeper, Langlois, crossed a canal. Its striking shape attracted Vincent, just as the windmills at home or at Montmartre had loomed against an open sky. Its sturdy wooden framework presented an image not unlike a weaver's loom.

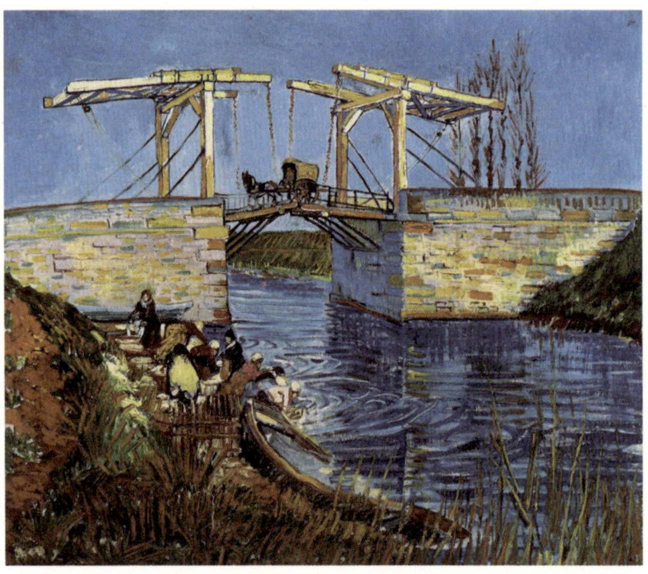

Langlois Bridge with Washerwomen, 1888

"I've found a funny thing of a kind I'm not going to do every day. It's the drawbridge with a little yellow carriage and group of washerwomen, a study in which the fields are a bright orange, the grass very green, the sky and the water blue."

He made many drawings of the bridge, from all sides. Just as he had viewed the bridge in Nieuw-Amsterdam, he placed it centre canvas, giving the everyday landmark a bold dignity.

Arles, itself, with its variety of buildings from many ages, hardly attracted him. He found the rich carving on the façade of the great pilgrimage church, St Trophime, *"so cruel, so monstrous, like a Chinese nightmare."* For him it belonged to another world, as distant as Roman Gaul. The ancient amphitheatre dominated an area in the centre of the town, yet he found the crowds who attended bullfights there more appealing than its architecture.

"By the way, have seen bullfights in the arena, or rather, simulated fights, seeing that the bulls were numerous but nobody was fighting them. But the crowd was magnificent, great multi-coloured crowds. One on top of the other on 2, 3 tiers, with the effect of sun and shade and the shadow cast by the immense circle."

Wherever he went, Vincent found colour. The colour juxtapositions he had learned in Paris, that banished his northern earth tones, now became fixtures on his palette. Despite the weight and awkwardness of his materials, he walked out into the country, attracted by its beauty, where he spent many daylight hours. However, when he returned to the Hotel Carrel, no welcome awaited him. The owners objected to his paintings and equipment that took up far too much space. Vincent knew he would have to move. By the beginning of May he had found another place.

This was the right-hand-side of a yellow-painted house, uninhabited and in a bad state of neglect. It stood near the river on the corner of a busy street overlooking a public garden. The drab area was just outside the old city walls, not far from the station and conveniently near Arles' brothel district. It had four small rooms and a back kitchen, with use of a lavatory next door. Excitedly, Vincent wrote to Theo about it.

Sketch of the Yellow House in letter to Theo, 1888

"Now what I'd like to do would be to furnish a room, the one on the first floor, to be able to sleep there. The studio, the store, will remain here for the whole of the campaign here in the south, and that way I have my independence from petty squabbles over guest-houses, which are ruinous and depress me."

The idea of having a fixed place, rented in his own name, raised Vincent's spirits. For the time being, until the house was refurbished, he took a room at the nearby Café de la Gare. Now he could plan the organisation of the yellow-painted house. He believed he might even achieve his dream of sharing a studio with another like-minded painter. Theo would provide for any such artistic enterprise, to ensure its success.

"I'm still convinced that nature here is just what's needed to do colour. And so it's more than likely that I won't move from here.... If necessary, I could live at the new studio with someone else, and I'd very much like to. Perhaps Gauguin will come to the south."

At first a tentative correspondence took place between Vincent and Gauguin, who was ill in Brittany, unable to work. The more Vincent clung to his idea, the more he entreated Theo to support the ailing Gauguin.

"Because loneliness, worries, vexations, the need for friendship and fellow-feeling not sufficiently met, that's what's very bad, the mental emotions of sadness or disappointments undermine us more than riotous living: us, that is, who find ourselves the happy owners of troubled hearts."

As the summer approached, Vincent took time to further explore
the surrounding landscape and soon discovered the region of the
Camargue that was once covered by the sea. This wild wetland,
south of Arles, had changed its nature over centuries not only due to
the sea's recession, but also to the flow of the Rhone. Flat marshland
of lagoons drained by dykes reminded Vincent of Drenthe. He even
compared it to a Ruisdael painting. Unlike the north, it was home to
roaming horses, bulls and colourful flamingos.

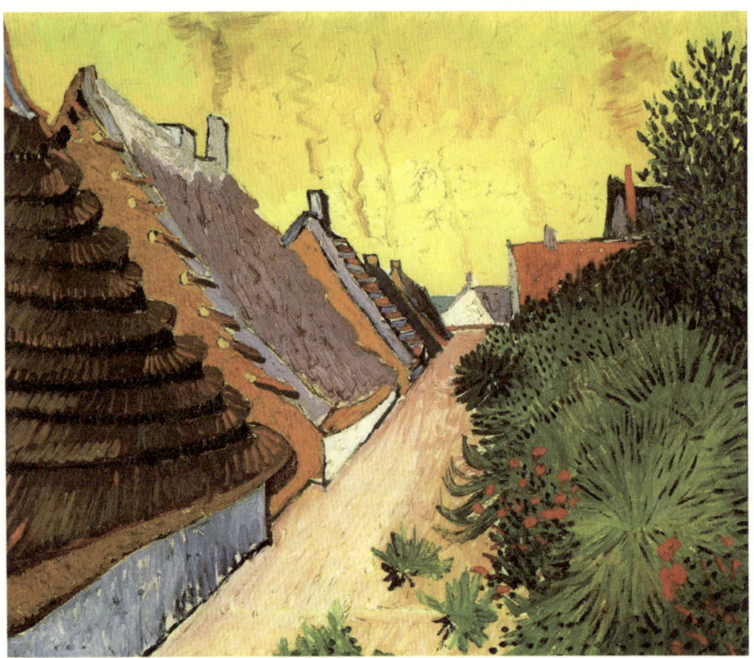

Street in Saintes-Maries-de-la-Mer, 1888

He drew and painted the striking homes of guardian herdsmen –
sturdy white-washed cottages with steep, thatched roofs that stand
as bold motifs on a canvas dominated by bright colouring.

Here, a journey of five hours in a carriage, was the Mediterranean.
Saintes-Maries-de-la-Mer owed its name to the legendary arrival on
a raft of the three Maries from the Holy Land. Once a year, in May,
gypsies came here on pilgrimage, paying homage to Sarah, the
servant who accompanied the Maries. Vincent painted the village
on a canvas placed vertically to provide a narrow view centred on
the twelfth-century church surrounded by encircling houses. The
church, which Vincent enlarged, looked out across the sea and was at
one time adapted to become a fortress. The buildings are coloured
orange, complementing the lavender-filled fields of
the foreground.

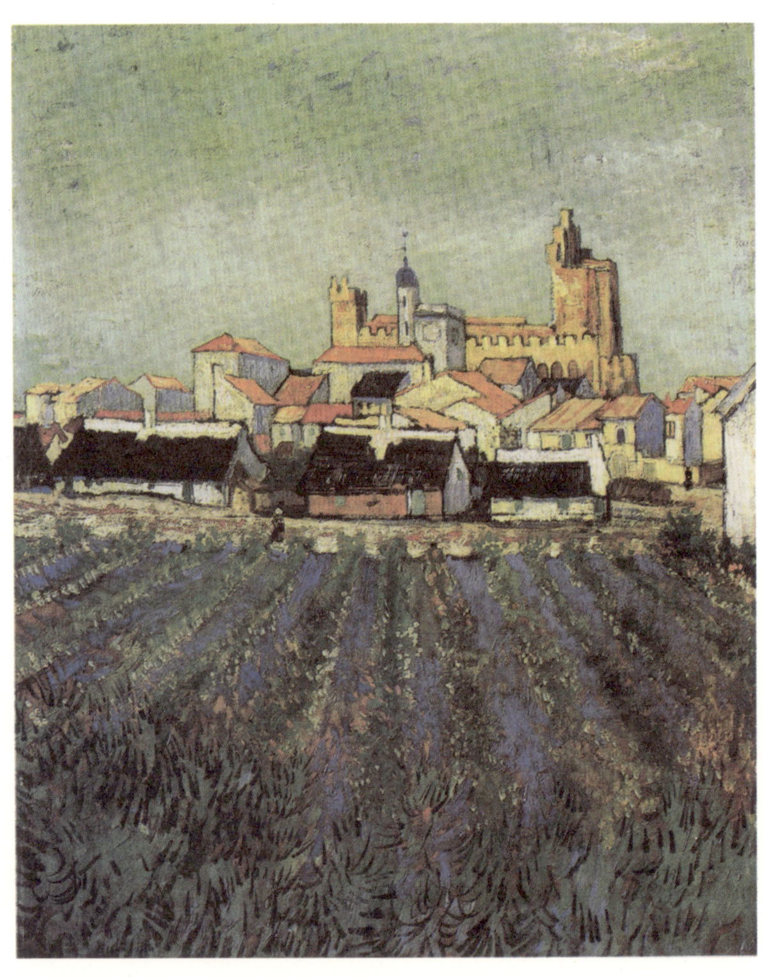

View of Saintes-Maries-de-la-Mer, 1888

One night Vincent walked on the deserted shore and saw the starlit sky as if it were filled with coloured jewels. He felt sure he would one day paint such a sky. For now, the seashore attracted him and in the early morning it was the scene of great activity.

"On the completely flat, sandy beach, little green, red, blue boats, so pretty in shape and colour that one thought of flowers; one man boards them, these boats hardly go on the high sea – they dash off when there's no wind and come back to land if there's a bit too much."

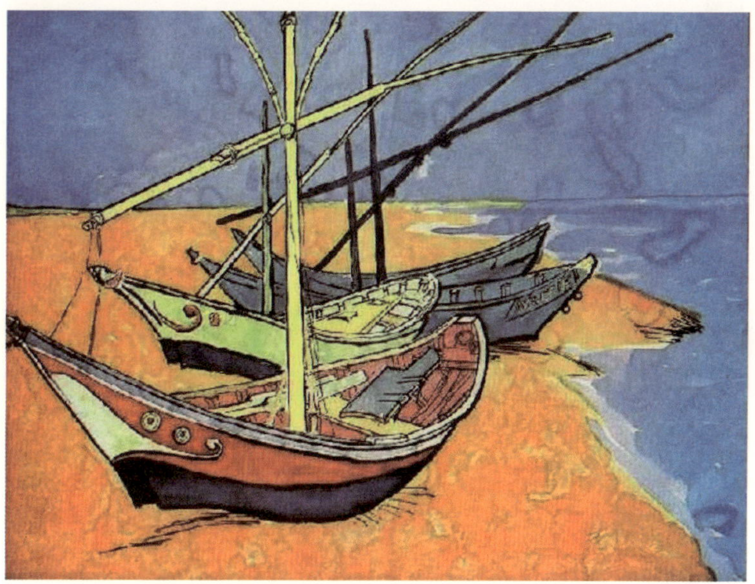

Fishing Boats on the Beach at Saintes-Maries-de-la-Mer, 1888

Vincent repeatedly drew and painted the beach in different weathers.
The vivid coloured boats stand still, casting no shadow on the sand.
The diagonal lines of their helms and masts create a busy pattern. The
lack of shaded perspective, only flat planes of colour, are reminiscent
of Japanese prints. One of the boats he named 'Amitié' – Friendship.

Back in the vicinity of Arles, Vincent often walked to a striking ruined
abbey that stood on raised rocky ground. The hillside of Montmajour
looked out over a wide, cultivated plain.

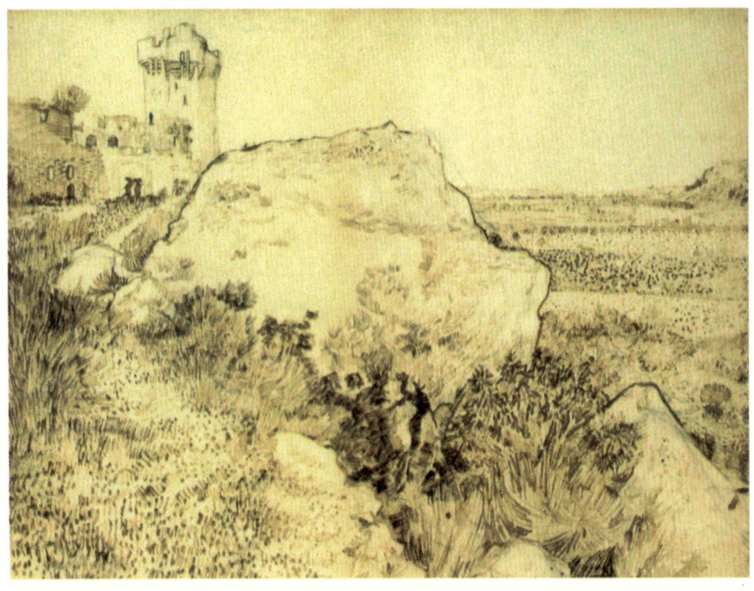

Hill with the Ruins of Montmajour, 1888

He drew the towering monument but also made studies of all that grew on the dry earth, notating textural variations with his unusual pen. This he had made from reeds and it enabled him to pursue a drawing style that could record the individuality of many natural motifs. He turned the nib of the reed pen in different ways, with varying pressure, and so achieved a detailed depiction of the unique terrain, so unlike his homeland.

Despite the summer's heat, Vincent painted the land now bursting with blazing colour. Harvest fields were animated by peasants at work. He found places to pitch his easel, by the road or high up on rocky spurs. With the sun's arrival the scenes that had once resembled the north were now filled with dazzling Provençal light. He worked furiously and very fast, sometimes creating two paintings a day.

"What strikes me here and what makes painting here attractive to me is the clarity of the air, you can't know what that is because it's precisely what we don't have at home – but an hour's distance one can make out the colour of things, the grey-green of olive trees and the grass green of the meadow, for instance, and the pink-lilac of ploughed land; at home we see a vague grey line on the horizon; here the line is sharp and the shape recognisable from far, far away. This gives an idea of space and air."

The plain of La Crau stretched out from the ruins of Montmajour. Vincent drew the wide expanse of complex field patterns with his reed pen, notating every variant of life with its quill.

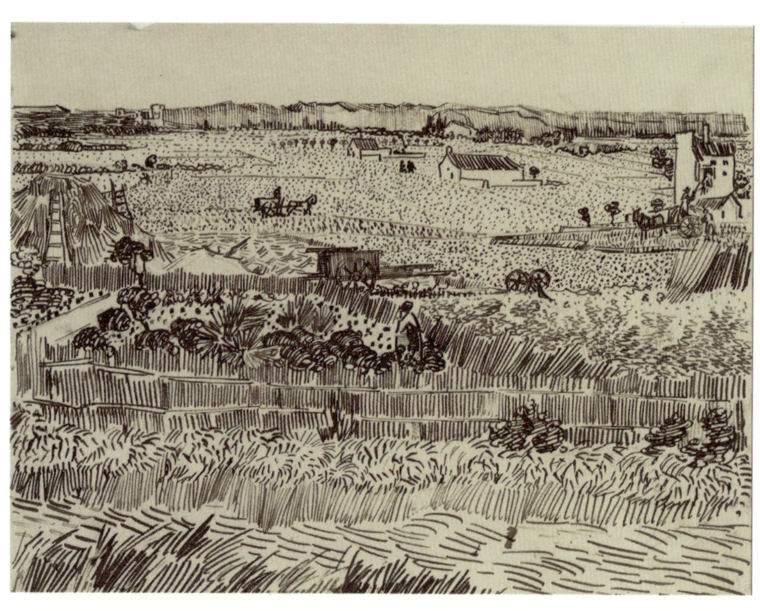

The Harvest (for Emile Bernard), 1888

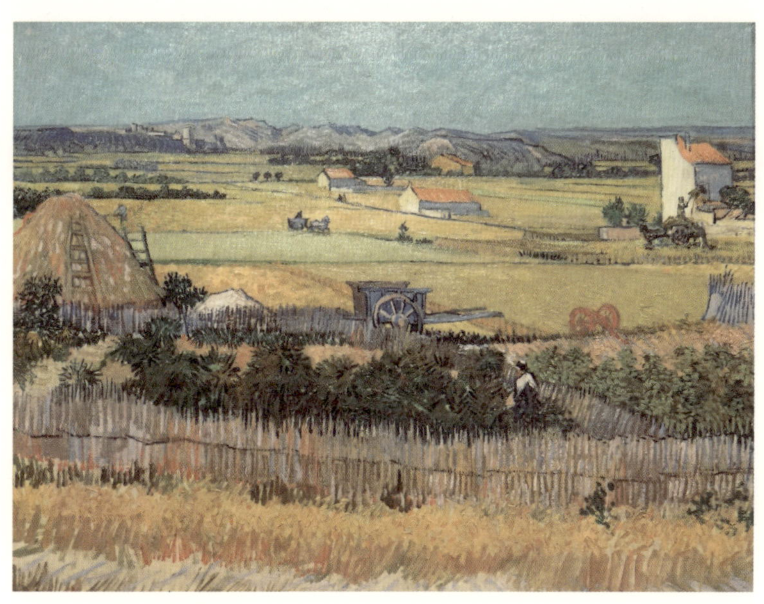

The Harvest, 1888

He repeated his masterly drawing style in meticulous painted brushwork. The horizon line of the Alpilles range of mountains lies high up on the canvas. The flat plain of brilliant yellow patchwork fields reaches out to the distant peaks. Nothing is in shadow. The single motifs of carts, wheels, shapely red rooftops and ladders each take their place in the wide view. None of the peasants are singled out for attention, but merge into the working scene as part of their land. Yellow, blue, green and red reverberate across the canvas.

"But during the harvest my work has been no easier than that of the farmers themselves who do this harvesting. Far from my complaining about it, it's precisely these moments in artistic life, even if it's not the real one, that I feel almost as happy as I could be in the ideal, the real life."

Although he achieved much, working alone with nature, Vincent still hoped to pursue portraiture. People in Arles were reluctant to pose for him but in a few portraits he established a bold frontal view of his sitters and lavished on them fine combinations of colour.

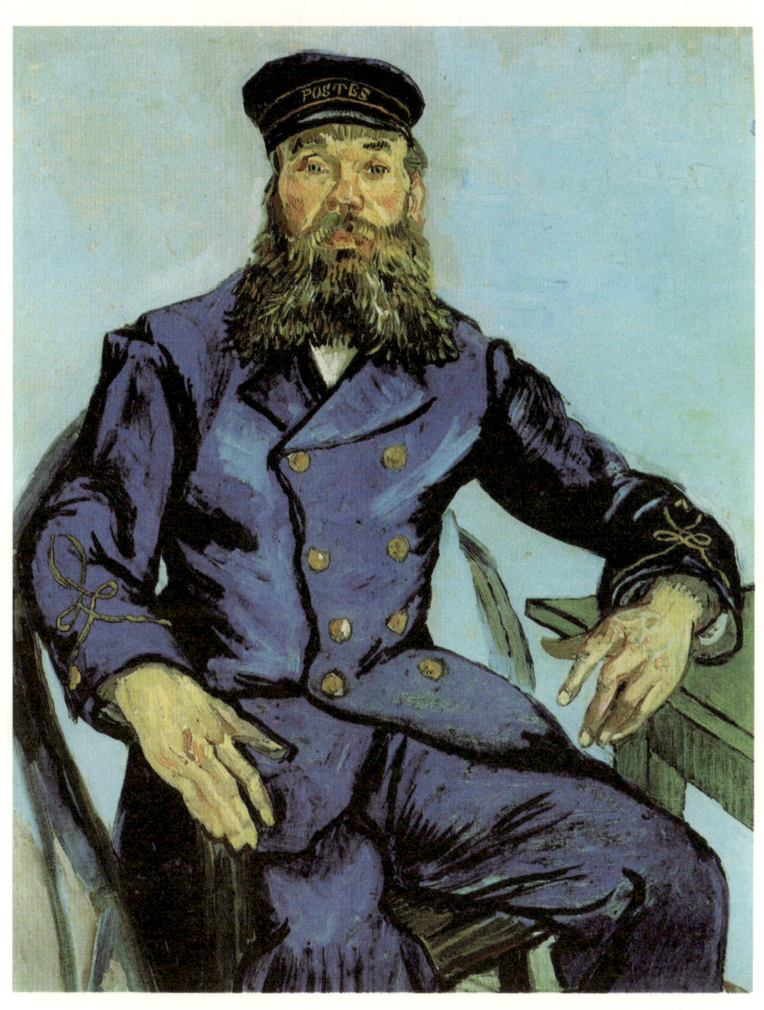

Postman, Joseph Roulin, 1888

Vincent, the compulsive writer of letters, received many in return. He also sent large parcels of his work up to Paris. It was not long before he made the acquaintance of a postal official, Mr Roulin, who worked at the train station. In time he painted his entire family in startling portraits where colour, carefully contrived, leaps off the canvas. An early portrait is a study in blue, where the postman's dark jacket and cap are highlighted by contrasting yellow stitching and buttons. The green of the table is picked out in his shapely beard and expressive face that reveals his strong personality. Vincent claimed he was an old Socrates, a raging republican and a more interesting man than most.

While in Arles, Vincent made advances in both portraiture and landscape painting as he developed a unique and dynamic style based on keen observation, sure draughtsmanship and a delight in colour. In Brittany, Gauguin also explored his own potential in scenes of Breton life. When he complained he was amongst a 'band of boors' and suggested coming south, Vincent was overjoyed.

"The fact remains that provided we lived in harmony and with an understanding not to quarrel, we'd gain a firmer position as far as reputation goes. Each of us living alone, we live like madmen or criminals, in appearance at least, and to some extent in reality too."

Throughout the summer Gauguin failed to give a firm date for his arrival, but Vincent remained busy. He continued to observe the brilliance of flowers in bloom. He began to paint sunflowers. These were not new to him, but here they were to become a repeated subject that he explored in several combinations of colours.

"Well, if I carry out this plan there'll be a dozen or so panels. The whole thing will therefore be a symphony of blue and yellow. I work on it all these mornings, from sunrise. Because the flowers wilt quickly and it's a matter of doing the whole thing in one go."

Money remained a continual burden placed at Theo's feet. Gauguin, who was also impoverished and with a large family to support, was already surrounded by painters in Brittany, including Bernard. Vincent was worried that the two were combining forces. Would Gauguin send someone else in his place? Trying not to anticipate rejection, Vincent threw himself into further work. He painted the café where he lived – an alarming portrait of his lodgings and its down-at-heel customers.

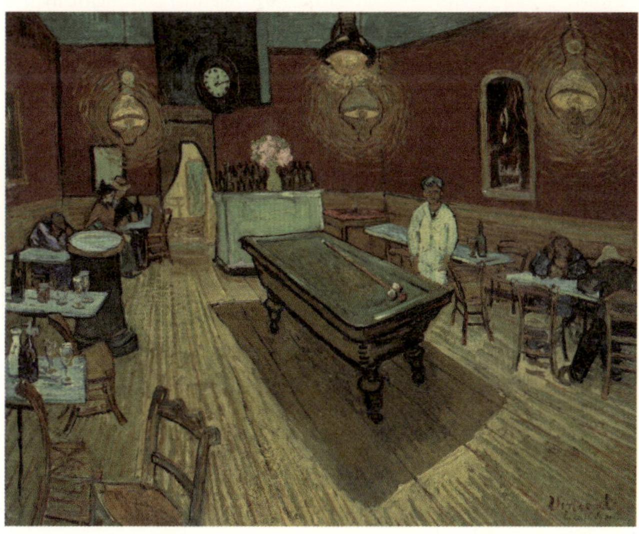

The Night Café, 1888

"I stayed up to paint, going to bed during the day. It often seems to me that the night is much more alive and richly coloured than the day ... the painting is one of the ugliest I've done.... I've tried to express the terrible human passions with the red and green."

This was no home, but the nightly scene at the café had struck him and he wanted to express that feeling. When he searched for hope, he reworked an image taken from Millet – the sower – and repeated it often, bathed in Provençal sunlight.

Nature restored his spirits, as did the near completion of the yellow-painted house. It was to be the centre of his creative world. At last, in mid-September, he was able to move in. Much of his energy was now placed in preparing the house for Gauguin's anticipated arrival. The spare room, naturally, could also be used by Theo.

"The room where you'll stay then, or which will be Gauguin's if Gauguin comes, will have a decoration of large yellow sunflowers on its white walls. Opening the window in the morning, you see the greenery in the gardens and the rising sun and the entrance of the town."

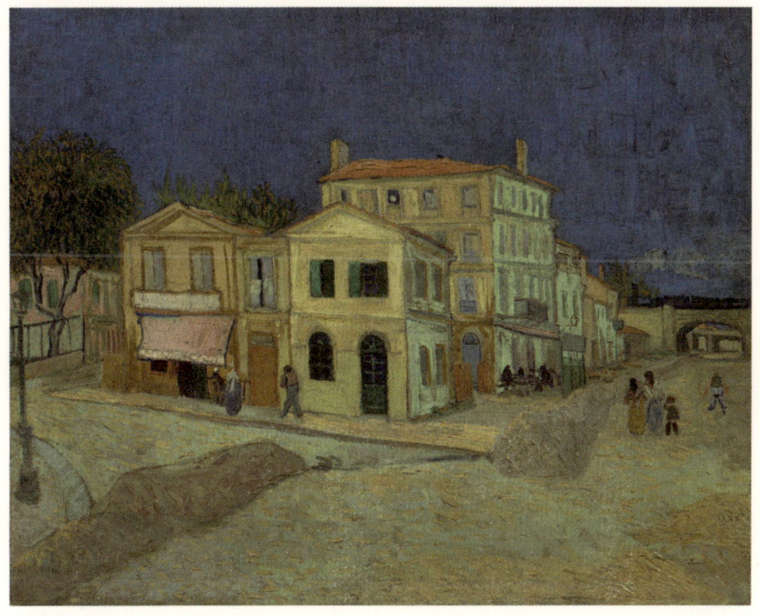

The Yellow House, 1888

A short distance from that entrance, at the edge of the gardens, was the river. For some time Vincent had planned to paint the sky at night and wondered how to do this without light. Here he stood on the banks of the Rhone beneath a street gas lamp and stared up into a sky filled with stars. He created a dazzling night sky.

"The sky is green-blue, the water is royal blue, the areas of land are mauve. The town is blue and violent. The gaslight is yellow, and its reflections are red gold and go right down to the green bronze. Against the green-blue field of the sky the Great Bear has a green and pink sparkle whose discreet paleness contrast with the harsh gold of the gaslight. Two small coloured figures of lovers in the foreground."

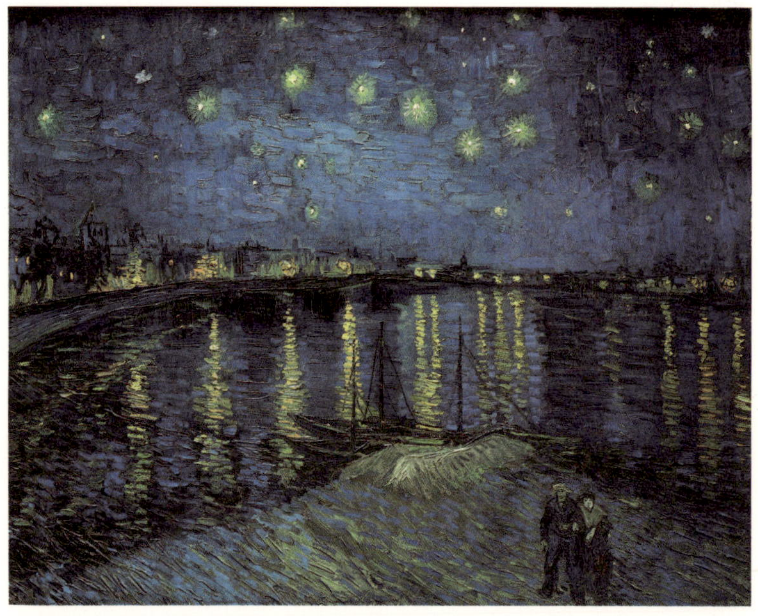

Starry Night Over the Rhone, 1888

The night is not threatening. He included the foreground lovers as he often added pairs of people to animate a scene. By now he believed no such lover would be his.

Vincent still waited for Gauguin. The house was decorated, the rooms complete, the sunflower paintings were hung on his guest's bedroom wall. When Theo was left a legacy on Uncle Cent's death, it provided the fare for Gauguin's journey south. Yet Vincent hardly knew this man on whom all his dreams for working together were fixed.

Gauguin had spent many childhood years in Peru. He claimed descent from people with 'savage' blood. Before the age of twenty he had sailed twice across the Atlantic and once round the world as a merchant seaman. When he married, he worked in the Paris Stock Exchange. He was the father of five children. Gauguin was a proud and confidant man who gave up everything to become an artist – and was admired by those who, like Vincent, were trying to see their modern, post-Impressionist ideas recognised.

At 4.00am on 23 October 1888, Gauguin arrived in Arles. On the same day Theo sold one of his Breton paintings. From the start there was a disparity between Vincent and his guest. It did not take long for both of them to discover their work was very different, conceived from opposing ideas. Gauguin, who told tales of his exotic travels, did not take to Arles – 'the filthiest place in the south', and compared it unfavourably with Brittany. However, Vincent, so thrilled to have him there, made no complaints.

Gauguin painted the same café interior as Vincent's, but peopled it with brothel characters, including the owner's wife, Mme Ginoux, who willingly sat for him. He worked slowly, with attentive thought, rather than with the speed of Vincent's self-expression. His paint was applied in measured strokes, layer upon layer. Almost as soon as he arrived, he bought 20m of coarse jute sacking, much cheaper than canvas. Vincent agreed to share it. They would also share the same subjects.

"At the moment he's working on some women in a vineyard, entirely from memory, but if he doesn't spoil it, or leave it there unfinished, it will be very fine and very strange."

Gauguin's wine harvest showed a pensive, disgruntled woman distantly based on a Peruvian mummy he had seen in a museum. His harvesters wore Breton costumes. A sinister dark-clothed figure appeared to the left of the canvas. Gauguin believed one should dream before nature, not copy it. He called the painting Human Miseries.

Vincent observed Provence – he drew or painted subjects that he saw before his eyes. His own vineyard shows peasants out in the open air, their grape-picking work identifiable, a large, round sun lending a warm light across the scene.

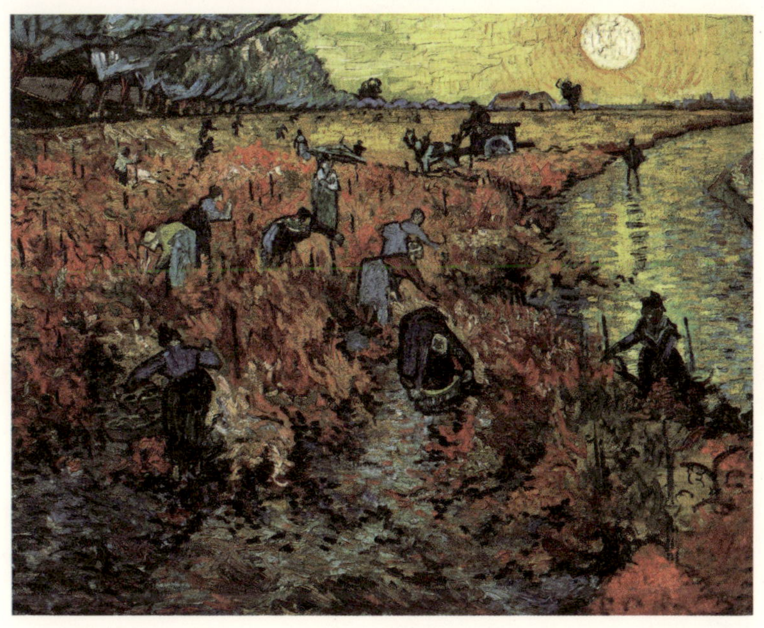

Red Vineyards, 1888

When the two artists went down beyond the town's old walls, they painted different views of Les Alyscamps, the ancient burial ground, now dazzling with autumn colouring.

"These tree-trunks, like pillars, line an avenue where old Roman tombs coloured lilac-blue are lined up to right and left. Now the ground is covered as if by a carpet with a thick layer of orange and yellow leaves – fallen. Some are still falling, like snowflakes. And in the avenue dark figurines of lovers. The top of the painting is a very green meadow and no sky, or almost none."

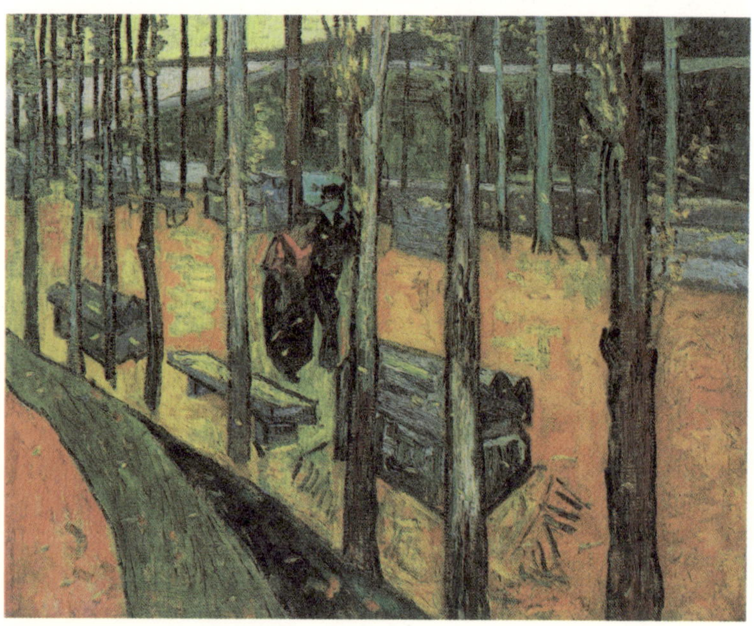

Falling Autumn Leaves, 1888

130

Vincent delighted in the change of seasons and made several paintings there. He was able to create a harmony of complementaries in the natural colouring of fallen leaves and the meadow. His composition, seen through tree trunks, was a device used in Japanese prints.

Gauguin stepped up on the bank and painted a view down to the church at the end of the walkway. Three figures stand in its centre. He called it Landscape or Three Graces with the Temple of Venus. He cared little for complementaries and preferred to concoct his own colour schemes.

Gauguin took up the cooking in the yellow house, for which Vincent was grateful. His admiration went further when he began to follow Gauguin's ideas.

"Gauguin gives me courage to imagine, and the things of the imagination do indeed take on a more mysterious character."

Soon he would attempt to paint a dream. As he followed Gauguin's lead, he looked not at the real world but back into his past. He remembered a previous home and its garden – in Etten – and wrote to Wil about his new canvas.

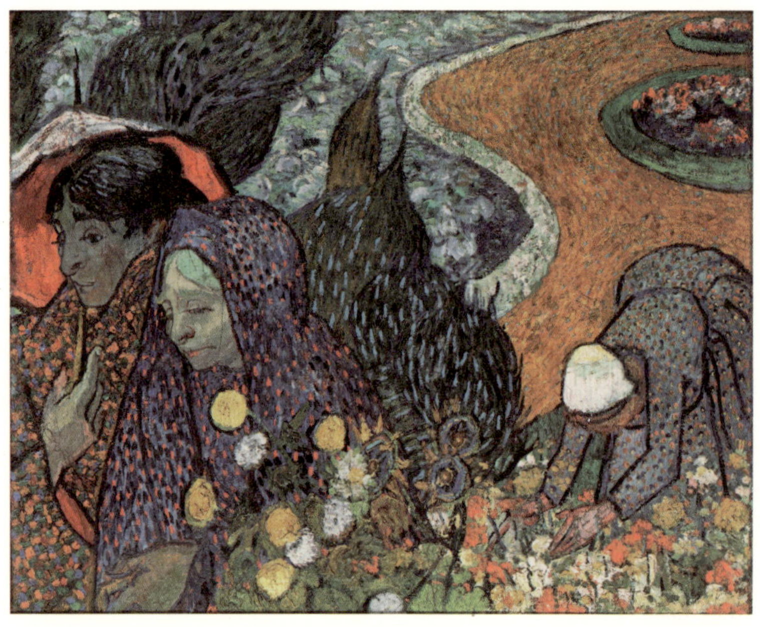

Memory of the Garden at Etten, 1888

"I know it isn't perhaps much of a resemblance, but for me it conveys the
poetic character and the style of the garden as I feel them. In the same
way, let's suppose that these two women walking are you and our mother.
Let's even suppose then that there may be not the slightest, absolutely
not the slightest vulgar and fatuous resemblance, the deliberate choice
of colour, the dark violet violently blotched with the lemon yellow of the
dahlias, suggests Mother's personality to me...."

Vincent was falling under Gauguin's spell and he craved his friend's approval. He described every painting he worked on – of interest to Theo whose display of Gauguin's work was being admired on the company's mezzanine floor. However, Vincent became more and more anxious, fearing that Gauguin's potential success – and their differences – would send him away.

By December, Gauguin was ready to go. 'Taking everything into account I am obliged to return to Paris,' he wrote to Theo. 'Vincent and I can absolutely not live side by side without trouble, as a result of incompatibility of temperament, and both he and I need tranquillity to work.'

Vincent acknowledged their differences.

"I myself think that Gauguin had become disheartened by the good town of Arles, by the little yellow house where we work and above all by me."

However, Gauguin did not leave. As a diversion from the tiny house where they lived and worked, the two made an excursion 70km west to Montpellier to visit the Musée Fabre that they both enjoyed, but this was not sufficient to heal their differences. After two months the whole venture – and Vincent's cherished dream – was coming to an end.

For weeks, unsure of Gauguin's intentions, Vincent showed symptoms of extreme nervous instability. He feared he would be left alone. It was Christmas. On 23 December, in a state of total mental collapse, Vincent cut off part of his ear. He walked to the nearby brothel and asked for it to be given to Gauguin's favourite prostitute. When he was found wounded the next day, Gauguin alerted Theo, who arrived as soon as he could and visited him in hospital. 'He seemed to be all right for a few minutes when I was with him,' Theo said later, '… but lapsed shortly afterwards into his brooding about philosophy and theology.'

Gauguin quickly returned to Paris.

Vincent's breakdown was characterised by hallucinations, silence, confusion and aggression, which was difficult to diagnose. On his admission to hospital, his most attentive doctor, Félix Rey (1867–1932), believed he should go to an asylum, as in Arles they were not equipped to deal with mental illness. The days passed, Vincent grew calmer and he was allowed home in early January. He told Theo how it had been.

"During my illness I again saw each room in the house at Zundert, each path, each plant in the garden, the views round about, the fields, the neighbours, the cemetery, the church, our kitchen garden behind – right up to the magpies' nest in a tall acacia in the cemetery."

The childhood he had once known was never forgotten. It bound him to his brother. By now Jo Bonger had agreed to marry Theo, and their wedding was planned for April. In happier spirits, Vincent congratulated the couple. He also convinced himself that Gauguin was unstable and this had played a great part in his breakdown.

"At the bottom of our hearts good old Gauguin and I understand each other, and if we're a bit mad, so be it, aren't we all sufficiently deeply artistic to contradict anxieties in that regard by what we say with the brush?"

Once home again, Vincent wasted no time in returning to work, creating two paintings of himself with his bandaged ear as well as a portrait of Dr Rey. In full control of his brush, he carefully outlined the figure and placed it against a dazzling patterned wallpaper background, bringing together primary colours in a method that was now his accomplished portraiture style.

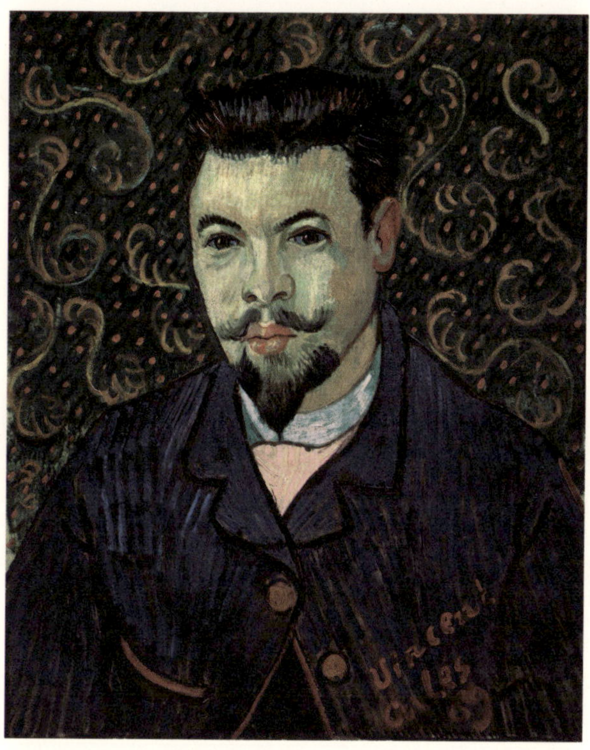

Portrait of Der Félix Rey, 1889

The frequent company of Roulin, the postal official, contributed towards a more settled time, and Vincent began a series of portraits of his wife, the new mother. These were entitled Lullaby. The idea came to him that they could be images of comfort to sailors at sea whenever they were homesick.

Although Dr Rey had advised less work and walks in the fresh air, Vincent suffered a second breakdown and was taken to hospital by police where he was placed in an isolation cell, under observation. There he was visited by a local Protestant pastor, the Rev. Frédéric Salles, who informed Theo of Vincent's condition. 'For three days he has thought he is being poisoned and just sees poisoners and victims of poison everywhere. The cleaning woman, who is showing considerable devotion in caring for him, faced with his more than abnormal condition, felt it her duty to tell others, and neighbours brought it to the attention of the police....'

The idea that he should be admitted to an asylum was again raised, but Dr Rey preferred to keep him in his care, to hope for progress and allow him to return to the yellow house during the day. This was a gesture towards some liberty for a man who was often lucid in thought. When a petition for his admission to an asylum was signed by thirty neighbours, fearful for their safety, the police again took Vincent away and boarded up the yellow house.

In March, Vincent had a welcome visitor – Signac, the painter who had spent much time with him in Paris the previous summer. He found Vincent 'in a perfect state of physical and mental health. We went out together yesterday afternoon and again this morning. He took me to see his paintings of which many are very good and all of them very intriguing....' Together they broke into the yellow house.

Vincent believed he was now a prisoner, but his physical health, under care, was improving. Dr Rey knew he should have meals at regular hours, a change from his usual excesses of coffee and alcohol. He also offered Vincent his own apartment as a place to live, near the Trinquetaille Bridge on the right bank of the Rhone. The previous year, Vincent, so interested in the structure of bridges, had painted the great metal and concrete landmark as a complex mass, dominating most of the canvas.

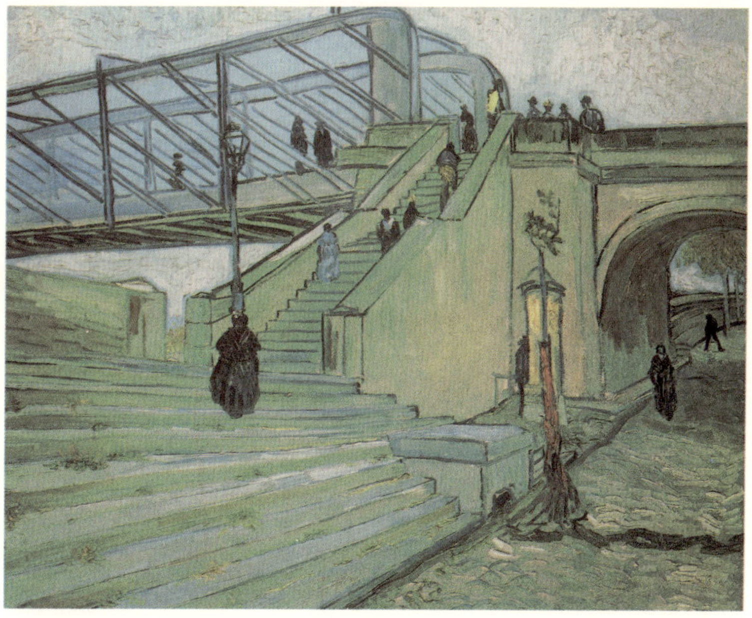

Trinquetaille Bridge, 1888

Vincent did not accept Dr Rey's offer, fearing to be alone. By late March he felt admission to an asylum, for a period of a few months, might restore him to complete health. He resented the opinion of the police, who had stated he was potentially a danger to public safety.

"If – let's say – I were to become definitively insane – certainly I don't say that it's impossible, in any case they should treat me differently, give me back the fresh air, my work, etc."

The Rev. Salles had visited an asylum not far away and recommended it to Theo. Knowing the significance of work for Vincent, Theo wrote to its director, asking if he could paint there. By the time the spring blossom had returned, Vincent held an optimistic outlook for the coming months, but before he left the hospital, he needed to commit this place to canvas.

"I'm working though, and have just done two paintings of the hospital. One is a ward, a very long ward with rows of beds with white curtains where a few figures of patients are moving.... And then, as a pendant, the inner courtyard. It's an arcaded gallery like in Arab buildings, whitewashed. In front of these galleries an ancient garden with a pond in the middle and 8 beds of flowers, forget-me-nots, Christmas roses, anemones, buttercups, wallflowers, daisies, etc.... So it's a painting chock-full of flowers and springtime greenery."

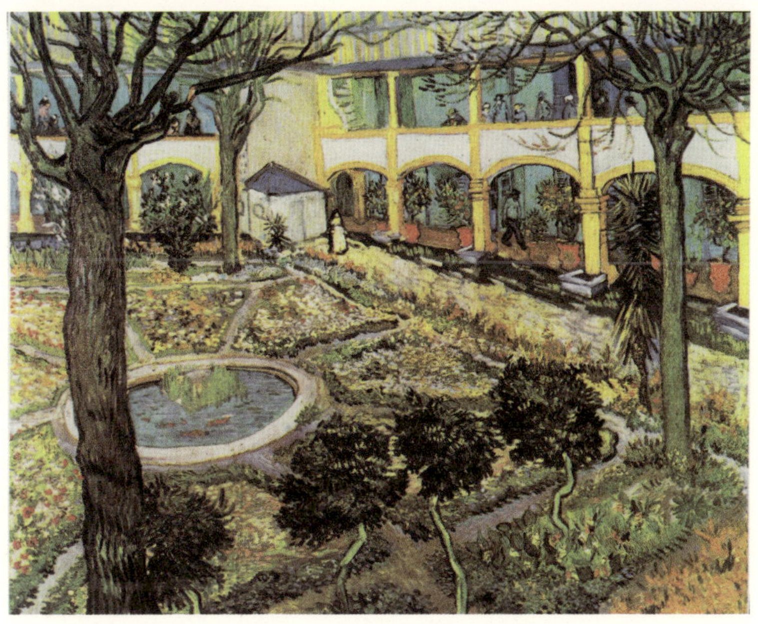

Garden of the Hospital at Arles, 1889

When he returned to the yellow house, to pack his work in crates for Paris and retrieve his belongings, he found it had been flooded. In his absence, much of his work had been spoiled. His dream was over.

"That had an effect on me, not only the studio having foundered, but even the studies which would have been the memories of it damaged, it's so final, and my urge to found something very simple but durable was so strong."

The distance from Arles to **SAINT-RÉMY** was some 25km. Vincent
took the train here in early May 1889, accompanied by the Rev. Salles.
The asylum was housed in large monastic buildings attached to an
old church, Saint-Paul de Mausole. This was named after a Roman
memorial mausoleum that stood near its gates. The beautiful site
that had attracted both ancient settlers and medieval monks was a
wide, sunlit valley stretching beneath the pale peaks of the Alpilles
mountains.

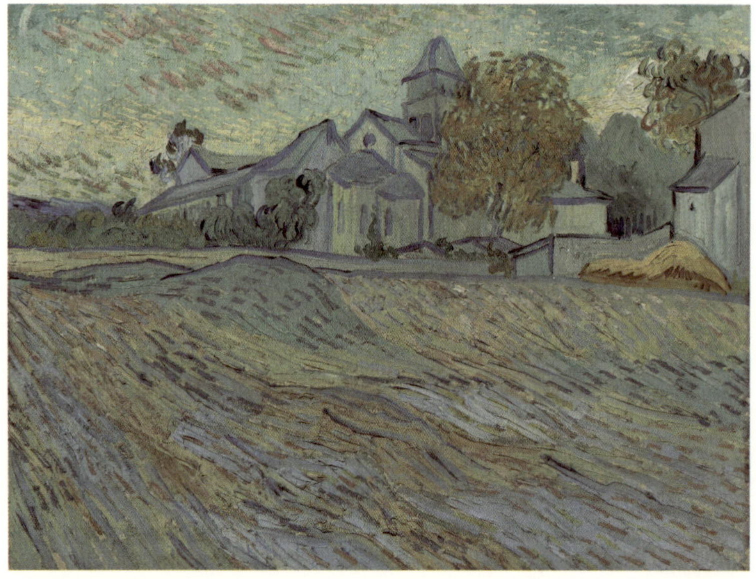

View of the Church of Saint-Paul-de-Mausole, 1889

140

Dr Théophile Peyron, an ophthalmologist who was once a doctor in the navy, was now to supervise Vincent's care. He gave him one of many empty bedrooms but also the use of a ground-floor area as his studio. During the day, Vincent was allowed to paint within the asylum's gardens.

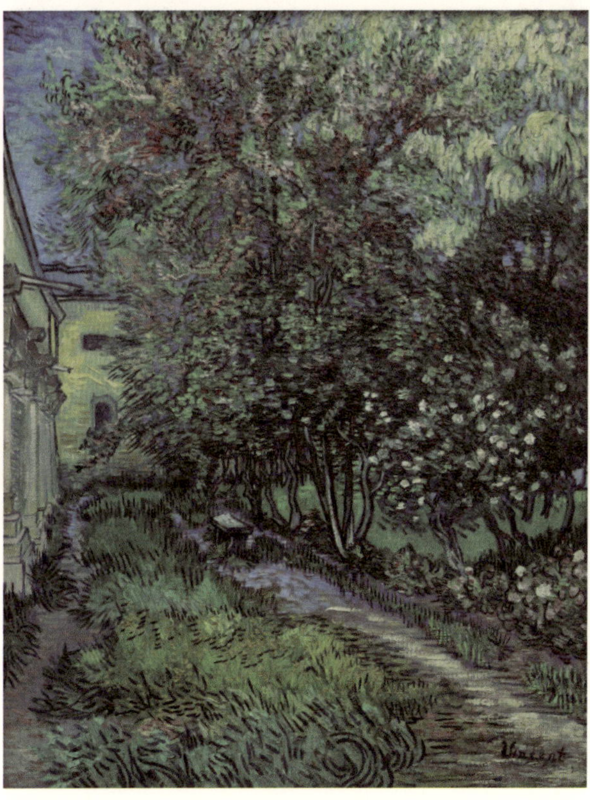

The Garden of St Paul Hospital, 1889

"Since I've been here, the neglected garden planted with tall pines under which grows tall and badly tended grass intermingled with various weeds, has provided me with enough work, and I haven't yet gone outside. However, the landscape of Saint-Rémy is very beautiful, and little by little I'm probably going to make trips into it."

Vincent was now undisturbed and in a safe environment. He explored the contained gardens, painting and drawing views of the hospital buildings, beds of irises in full bloom and even studied a small insect – the kind he had loved as a child.

"To paint it I would have had to kill it, and that would have been a shame since the animal was so beautiful."

The view from his barred window held none of the bustle of towns and cities he had known. He looked out over wheatfields that stretched to the lower slopes of the Alpilles. When he painted the mountains, with their soft shadows, he chose half tones in less bright shades than he had previously used.

By June, since he appeared content, he was given permission to go outside, accompanied by a warden. Now he could work among the olive groves that lay between the asylum's walls and the rising hills, as well as near brilliant yellow wheatfields.

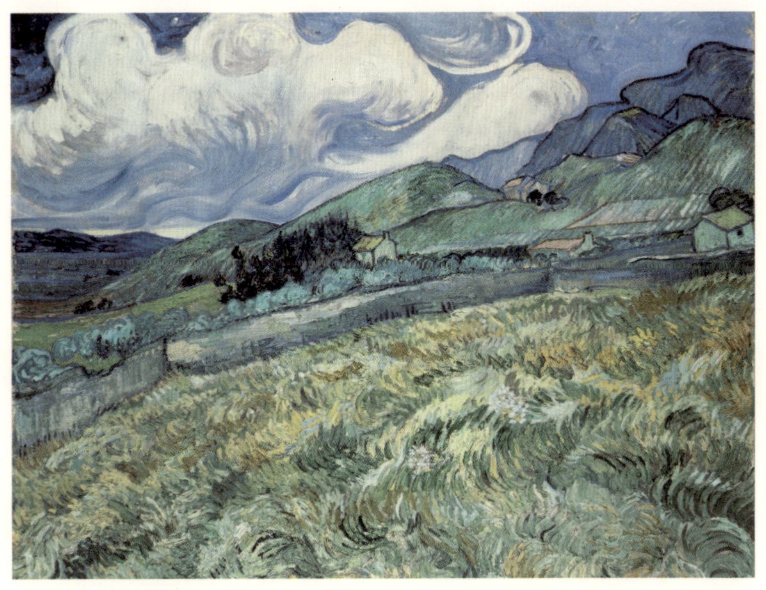

Landscape from St Remy, 1889

"I've just finished a landscape of an olive grove with grey foliage more or less like that of the willows, their cast shadows violet on the sun-drenched sand. Then yet another that depicts a field of yellowing wheat surrounded by brambles and green bushes. At the end of the field a little pink house with a tall and dark cypress tree that stands out against the distant purplish and bluish hills, and against a forget-me-not blue sky streaked with pink whose pure tones contrast with the already heavy, scorched ears, whose tones are as warm as the crust of a loaf of bread."

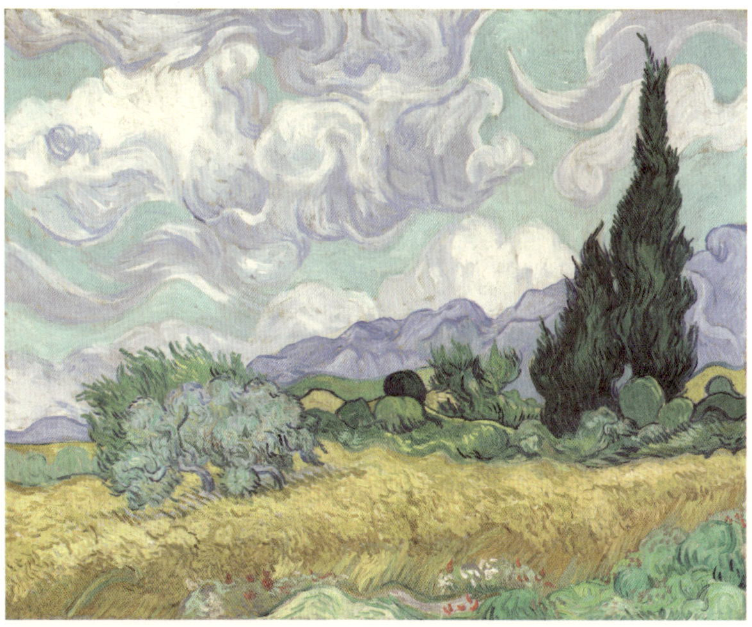

Wheat fields with Cypresses, 1889

Theo was less happy about the work Vincent produced in the summer, astonished by the bold, calligraphic strokes he applied to natural forms. Tall cypress trees, rocky hills and olive trees were now painted with swirling gestures of the loaded brush. When Vincent worked on another night sky filled with stars, they appeared like coiling lamps in unrestrained movement over a still, sleeping town.

Vincent read Theo's thoughts, as well as the latest news from Paris. Gauguin and his friends had organised an exhibition of their work. By now their combined effort to become recognised, even understood, Vincent found almost laughable. The effort could lead to madness. Still, he continued to send his finished work to Theo who never ceased to encourage him with the new motifs he had found in this beautiful part of Provence.

He looked out of his window and could not help comparing people in the fields to peasants of the north – the home that never left his thoughts. When he heard his youngest brother, Cor, was about to leave for South Africa, he reminded his mother of the pain of parting.

"Now, my dear mother, as regards the sorrow that we have and retain about parting and loss, it seems to me that it's instinctive, that without it we wouldn't be able to accept partings, and it will probably serve us on later occasions to recognise and find one another again."

In July, Vincent heard that Theo's wife, Jo, was pregnant. Unable to celebrate with his family at a distance, he bravely accepted his lot. This was thanks to being occupied, a true therapy that helped him survive an intolerable environment. He looked on his fellow inmates with compassion. Their treatment was little other than 'hydrotherapy'

– long hours spent in a bath. Vincent knew he needed to be there, but was guiltily aware of the expense it cost Theo, especially now he was going to become a father. However, his new liberty – undisturbed by the demands of daily survival – would surely make him better.

On one occasion he was allowed to return to Arles, to organise his belongings at the Café de la Gare. It was his first outing since being at Saint-Rémy and he was again accompanied by an attendant, for safety. Although he claimed the trip did him good, none of his old friends were there. The Rev. Salles was on holiday and the news of Dr Rey was vague. His closest friend, Roulin, the post official, now lived in Marseille.

Not long after this trip, Vincent found an extraordinary new location to paint, near the asylum, yet entirely hidden from view. An old limestone quarry had provided stone for the construction of the Roman town nearby. The sharp angles of its brutally cut rock surfaces, together with the vegetation that had grown there, gave him a choice of striking, sturdy motifs and a different kind of view, inwards, rather than to open country.

He set up his easel among the stones, but the fierce wind that swept at the quarry entrance sent these astray. While there, he felt the old symptoms of his illness return. In the dark green and ochre colours of the painting that he finished later, he claimed he found something sad.

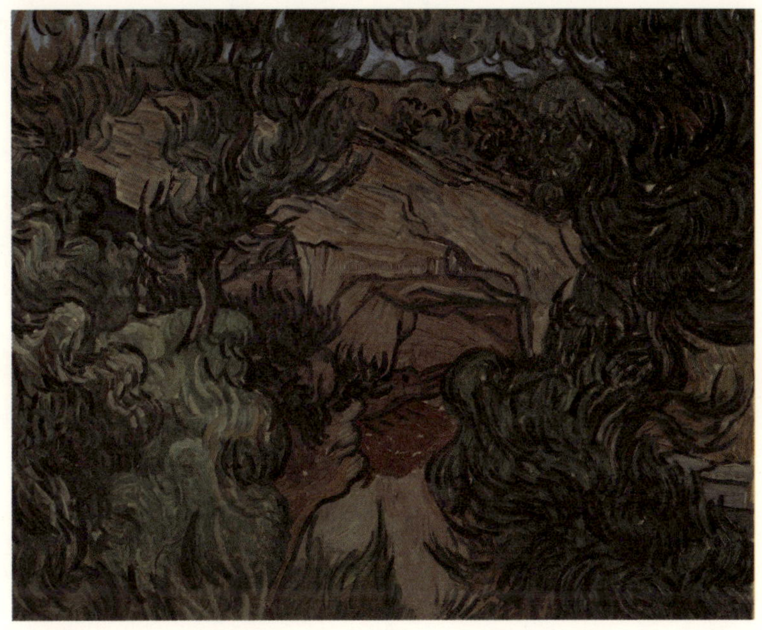

Entrance to a Quarry, 1889

From July through to August, Vincent suffered more attacks that left him with terrifying hallucinations, feelings of aggression followed by exhaustion and unconsciousness. Confined for safety, he was forbidden to paint and begged Theo to write to Dr Peyron, explaining that only activity would lead to his recovery.

"For these days without anything to do and without going into the room he allocated me for doing my paintings, are almost intolerable to me."

Vincent was very aware of the implications of his illness and was determined to overcome them with work. The asylum was no home – he found the old cloisters cold and unwelcoming. He criticised the few nuns who lived there for telling inmates about the virtues of a saint. By September, when he was allowed to work again, he felt he would do better in the north. The landscape of the south made him melancholy.

His home remained fixed in his memory. When he wrote to Theo about the new life he would have with a child, his advice returned them to the old days.

"So take your fatherhood as a good fellow from our old heaths would take it, those heaths that remain ineffably dear to us through all the noise, tumult, fog, anguish of the town, however timid our tenderness may be."

The beauty of the countryside restored him. The land was changing colour and as another grape harvest approached, he returned to this earlier theme. He had already retouched some canvases, but the idea of doing a series – 'Impressions of Provence' – now motivated him.

"Anyway, it's difficult to leave a land before having something to prove that one has felt and loved it."

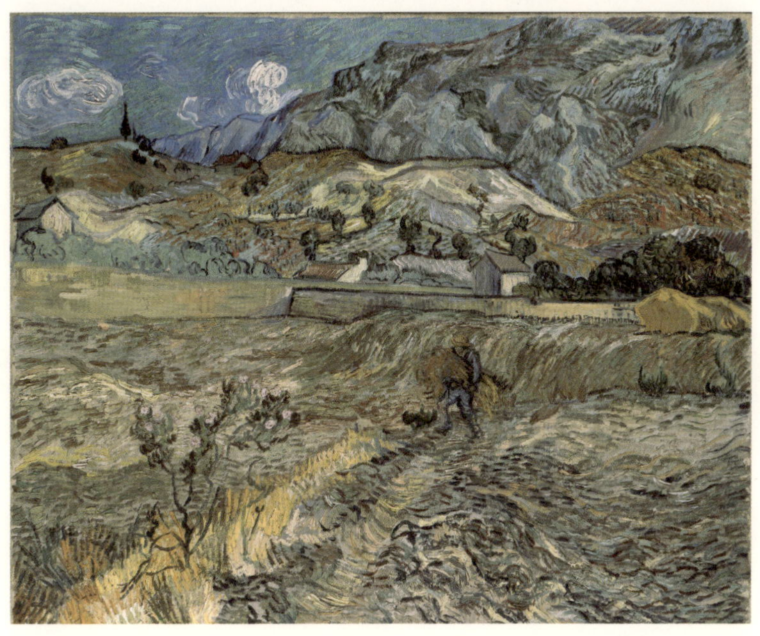

Landscape at St Remy (Enclosed Field with Peasant), 1889

Theo had been worried that Vincent was creating a deliberate style that 'takes away the real sentiment of things'. In another painting of the scene outside his window, differences between rocky hills, fields of wheat, vegetation, man-made walls and even clouds he painted with brushstrokes that resembled his accomplished drawing technique.

"I feel myself greatly driven to seek style, if you like, but I mean by that a more manly and more deliberate drawing."

He achieved a perfect balance of colours in his view that well represented the nature of Provence. Vincent was now at the height of his powers.

Once his state of mind improved, Theo urged him to work more instinctively and to be less concerned with ideas he exchanged with his fellow painters. To capture the natural world, as he saw and felt it, was the way forward. Both Gauguin and Bernard had told Vincent about their recent works on religious themes with the Garden of Olives as a subject they shared. Vincent's reply was to ridicule such themes – he was painting real olive groves, as he explained to Bernard.

"And if I haven't written for a long time, it's because, having to struggle against my illness and to calm my head, I hardly felt like having discussions, and found danger in these abstractions. And by working very calmly, beautiful subjects will come of their own accord; it's truly first and foremost a question of immersing oneself in reality again, with no plan made in advance, with no Parisian bias."

Thanks to Theo, an interest in Vincent's work was growing in Paris and even further afield. In November 1889, he was asked to exhibit work at the annual exhibition of Les Vingt, a forward-looking Belgian group of artists. Vincent accepted with pleasure and sent Theo six works he had created during his time in the south, two of which were of sunflowers.

The encouragement this gave Vincent was not enough to prevent renewed attacks of his illness. Christmas approached, as did the birth of Theo's baby, and it was nearly a year since the first traumatic event in Arles. Vincent worked furiously to combat a further episode, but when he was found in a distressed state and eating paint, he was confined once again.

Over several months the suggestion that he should go north, to a different institution, was explored. Vincent was becoming increasingly intolerant of the monotony of life in the asylum. He made light of his attacks, but knew that if he did not paint, there was little else to do.

"For the crowding together of all these lunatics in this old cloister is, I believe, becoming a dangerous thing in which one risks losing all the good sense one might still have retained. Not that I'm set on this or that by preference, I've become used to life here, but mustn't forget to try the opposite a little."

In January 1890, Vincent returned to Arles to visit his friends at the Café de la Gare. Soon after his return he suffered another attack, which, according to Dr Peyron, left him incapable of any kind of work. He responded to questions with incoherent words and once again was confined.

During the same month he became famous.

Theo had managed to have his paintings seen by people likely to be sympathetic towards modern trends. An article published in the Mercure de France, written by a writer and critic, Albert Aurier, poured lavish praise on Vincent's 'strange, intense and feverish' work. 'What

characterises his works as a whole is its excess ... of strength, of
nervousness, its violence of expressions. In his categorical affirmation
of the character of things, in his often daring simplification of form,
in his insolence in confronting the sun head-on, in the vehement
passion of his drawing and colour, even to the smallest details of his
technique, a powerful figure is revealed....'

When he recovered from his attack, Vincent was able to reply to
Aurier.

*"Thank you very much for your article ... which greatly surprised me. I like it
very much as a work of art in itself, I feel that you create colours with your
words; anyway, I rediscover my canvases in your article, but better than
they really are – richer, more significant. However, I feel ill at ease when I
reflect that what you say should be applied to others rather than to me."*

Aurier's praise drew further attention to Vincent's work. Only days
before her baby was born, Jo wrote to him to say how moved she was
by the article. She and his sister, Wil, who was staying with them, had
read it together. For Vincent, everything seemed to be happening in
Paris. Isolated, removed from his family and successful, he felt the need
to get away even more. In February he made another visit to Arles.

"He has had another attack, which prevents him from writing to you,
and which occurred following a visit to Arles,' wrote Dr Peyron to
Theo. 'I note that the crises are recurring more frequently and come
after each journey he makes outside this home. I was obliged to send
two men with a carriage to Arles to collect him, and it is not known
where he spent the night of Saturday to Sunday.'"

This time Vincent's recovery was long and difficult. He was unable to work – nor to read or write. For weeks he kept his head in his hands and, if spoken to, made signs that he preferred to be alone. The last painting he had touched was of branches of almond blossom to celebrate the birth of his nephew who was also named Vincent.

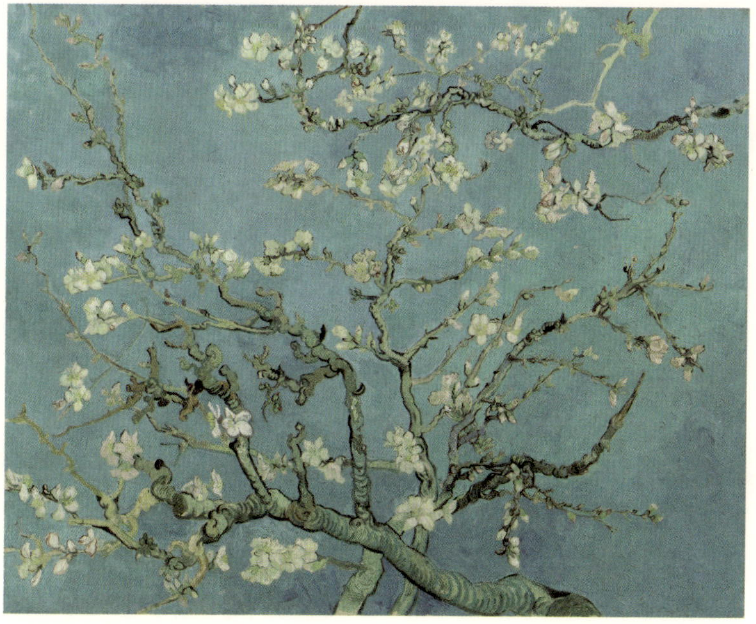

Almond Blossom, 1890

The simple subject, with its reference to Japan, was unlike anything he had done before. The fine delicacy of its handling was proof of his continuing achievement.

In March, some of his paintings were seen in an exhibition of Independents at another venue in Paris apart from the official Salon. As Vincent took slow steps towards recovery, entirely cut off from the Parisian art scene and confined in an asylum, his work was highly praised. Gauguin wrote to him, saying: 'I've looked most attentively at your works since we parted; first at your brother's place and at the Independents' exhibition. It's above all at this latter place that one can properly judge what you do, either because of things positioned beside each other, or because of the neighbouring works. I offer you my sincere compliments, and for many artists you are the most remarkable in the exhibition. With things from nature you're the only one there who thinks.'

Dr Peyron reported that Vincent's mental progress was spasmodic, that he descended into moments of confusion and sadness, but he felt sure he would recover. At the end of April, Vincent was back at work. In one scene of the Alpilles at sunset, he painted a pair of lovers strolling through the olive grove – the man has a shocking red head of hair and beard. This was wishful thinking, more like Gauguin's dreaming before nature. Another was a reminiscence of Brabant cottages beneath a dark, stormy sky. His homeland had never been forgotten.

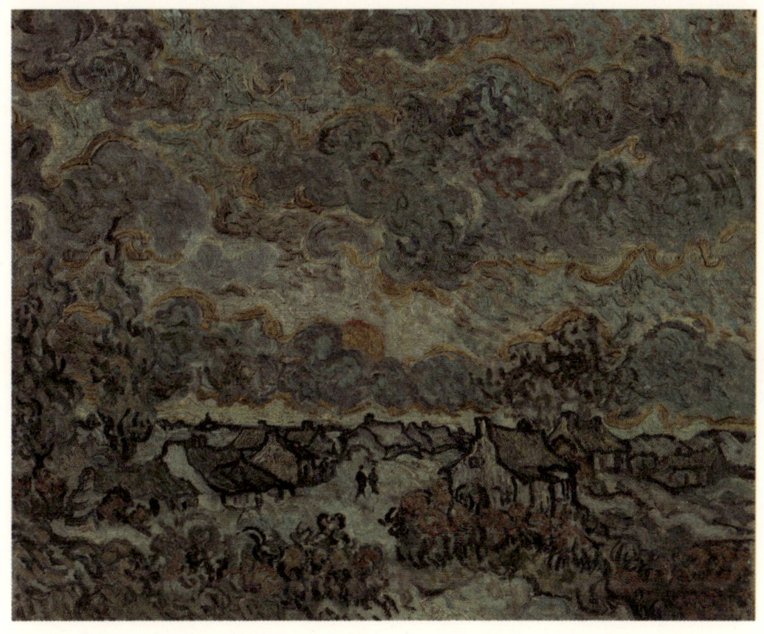

Reminiscence of Brabant, 1890

After a year's incarceration, there was little more the asylum could offer Vincent. Fortunately for him, it stood in a beautiful part of Provence that had given him courage as he tirelessly painted for survival. The sad lot of other inmates, who were not motivated as he was, troubled him, and his intolerance of living with them now contributed to a firm decision to leave. As long as he could continue painting, he would not object to moving away. His work had been recognised and he was capable of doing much more.

Dr Peyron pronounced Vincent cured. On the recommendation of the painter Camille Pissarro (1830–1903), a new doctor not far from Paris was found who was willing to look after Vincent.

"I think that it'll be best for me to go myself to see this doctor in the country as soon as possible; then we can soon decide if I'm going to lodge with him or temporarily at the inn; and thus we'll avoid an over-long stay in Paris, a thing that I would fear."

One of the last paintings Vincent did in Provence was the kind of dreaming that Gauguin practised – to whom he wrote about it.

"A last try – a night sky with a moon and without brightness, the slender crescent from the opaque projected shadow of the earth – a star with exaggerated brightness, if you like, a soft brightness of pink and green in the ultramarine sky where clouds run. Below a road bordered by tall yellow canes behind which are the blue low Alpilles, an old inn with orange lighted windows and a very tall cypress, very straight, very dark. On the road a yellow carriage harnessed to a white horse, and two late walkers. Very romantic if you like, but also 'Provençal' I think."

The inn was a thatched cottage, not found in Provence but common in his native land. The walking figures in the foreground are not lovers, but two men striding down a long road.

When his trunk was packed, Vincent looked out from the asylum at the fresh countryside that glowed from a shower of morning rain. How much more he would have done there, he thought, had he not been ill.

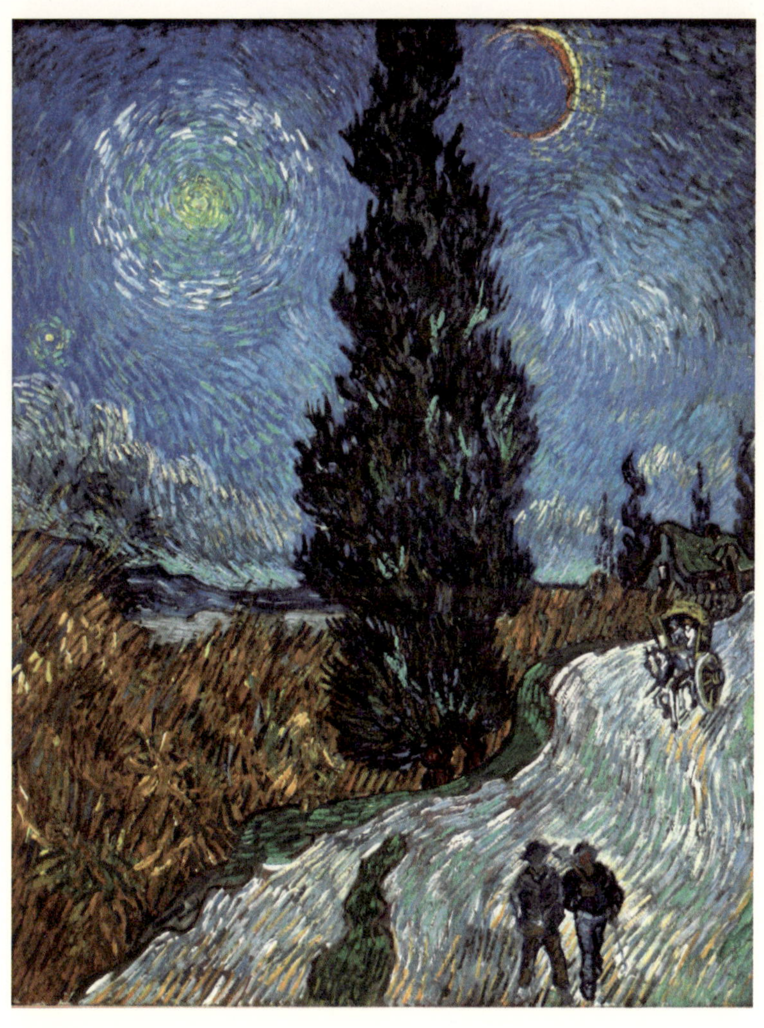

Road with Cypress and Star, 1888

In the mid-1870s the Impressionist artist Pissarro had worked with Cézanne in **AUVERS,** 30km northwest of Paris. Here was another rural spot that appealed to painters working out in the open air. Both artists knew Dr Paul Gachet (1828–1909), who had bought some of their paintings that included views of his house and the attractive village. Auvers lay on the banks of the river Oise. Behind a rise of houses and farms, tracks led up to a wide plateau of open countryside.

Vincent stayed in Paris after his long train journey and at Theo's new apartment he met, for the first time, Jo and his nephew. An old friend, Andries, Jo's brother, was also there. After his long period in the south, Vincent found Paris full of noise. He was very tired and fearing a relapse of his illness he eagerly left for Auvers after only three days.

"I've seen Dr Gachet, who gave me the impression of being rather eccentric, but his doctor's experience must keep him balanced himself while combating the nervous ailment from which it seems to me he's certainly suffering at least as seriously as I am. He directed me to an inn where they were asking 6 francs a day. For my part I've found one where I'll pay 3.50 a day. And until there's a change of circumstances, I think I ought to stay there."

The Auberge Ravoux was in the centre of the village, not far from the town hall. Vincent paid half board and was given a small attic room with storage space at the back of the house. As soon as he could, he began painting and went outside to record his first images of the picturesque village.

The style that Vincent had developed in the south now came north. His spontaneous brushstroke swept across the canvas, outlining homes with their thatched, sloping roofs and tracing the growth of rich meadows. Scenes of Auvers were filled with bright light.

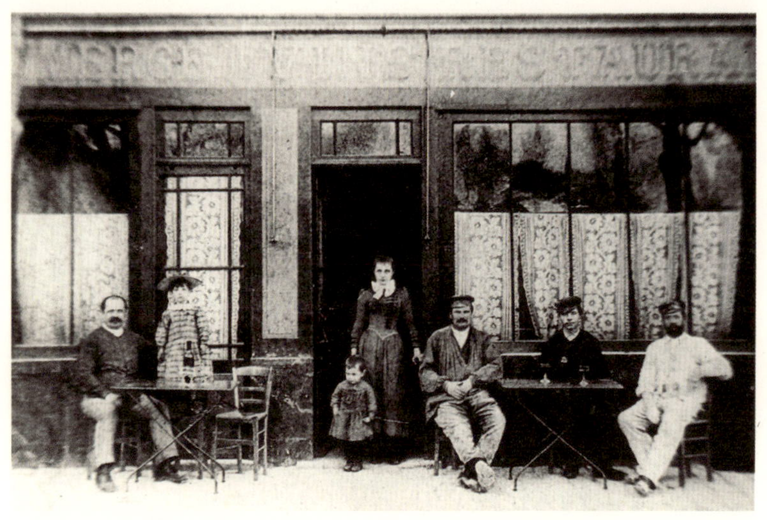

Auberge Ravoux, c. 1890

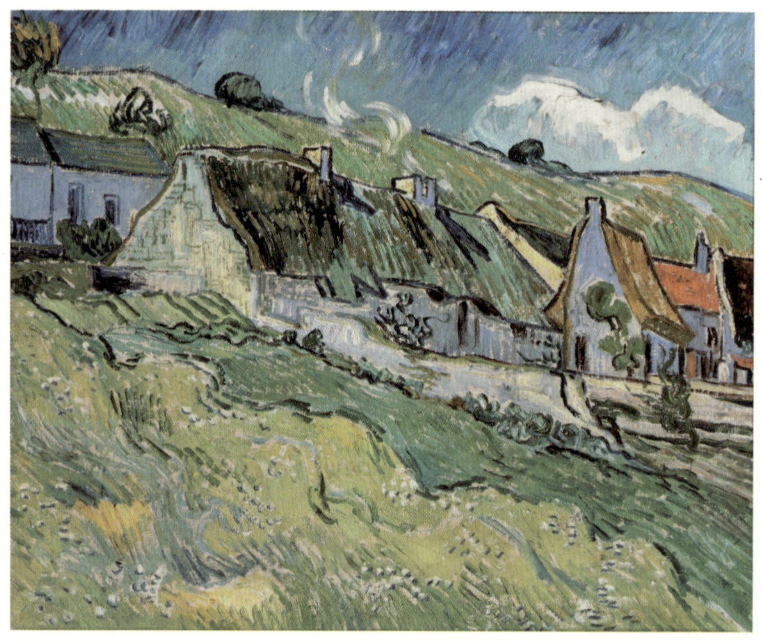

Thatched Cottages and Houses, 1890

Dr Gachet encouraged Vincent to paint with purpose and to think of the illness as a thing of the past. His encouragement was helpful and although Vincent considered him an 'odd fellow', he believed they would become good friends. This doctor was unlike others he had known – he talked about the many painters he knew, some of whom he had treated, and their work he admired. Vincent was particularly interested to know that the Barbizon painter, Daubigny, had lived in Auvers. Daubigny had died over ten years earlier, but his widow was still in the village at their house a short walk from the auberge.

As summer approached, Vincent felt the full benefit of being in the country. If he required their company, other painters were within reach in Paris. He received a letter from Dr Peyron at the asylum in Provence, who wrote: 'I see with pleasure that your health continues to be satisfactory, and that your life in the midst of this world of artists is spent more pleasantly than here.'

Staying in an auberge, however, was not being at home. A plan entered his mind – to bring Theo and his family to Auvers. Theo himself was unwell and Jo, on meeting Vincent, believed he was in better health than her husband. An added complaint was that Theo was now very dissatisfied at work. At first Vincent encouraged them to take frequent trips out of the city to see where he now was painting.

"I often think of you, Jo and the little one, and I see that the children here look well in the healthy fresh air. And yet it's difficult enough to raise them, even here, all the more is it rather terrible sometimes to keep them safe and sound in Paris on a fourth floor."

Vincent's plan soon developed into the idea of creating a real home in Auvers where all of them could live together.

For the moment he had the benefit of Dr Gachet's company. His large house, cluttered with antiques and that looked south over the river intrigued Vincent. Here he was frequently invited to eat large, family meals with the doctor, his son Paul and daughter Marguerite. Outside various species of poultry wandered at liberty in a flower-filled garden where Vincent hoped occasionally to work. He chose to paint the doctor's portrait in the garden.

"I would like to do portraits which would look like apparitions to people a century later. So I don't try to do us by photographic resemblance but by our passionate expressions, using as a means of expression and intensification of the character our science and modern taste for colour."

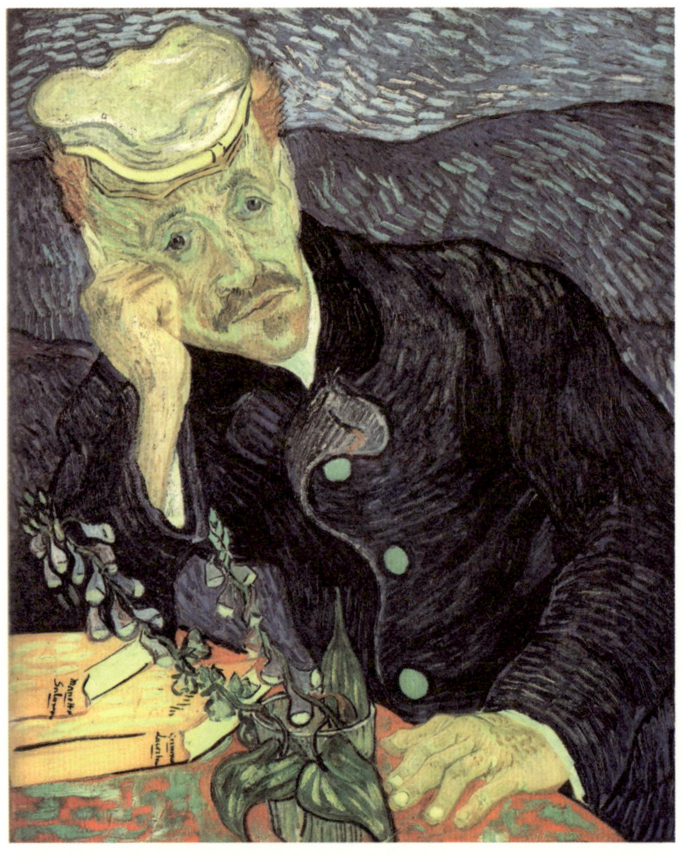

Portrait of Dr Gachet, June 1890 [1st version]

Dr Gachet sits not in a frontal position, facing outwards, but leaning
sideways in a thoughtful pose. He holds his head in his hand, as if
listening. On the table in a glass of water are sprigs of foxglove, a
reference to his interest in homeopathy. The addition of two books
adds further meaning to the portrait. Their titles are of novels by the
Goncourt brothers. In one, a country girl becomes corrupted and
dies in the city. The other is set in the world of bohemian artists. In
Vincent's portrayal of Dr Gachet, he becomes the means to an artist's
salvation, as does life in a place like Auvers.

Two versions of the portrait were done. Vincent explained to his sister
Wil what he intended in the portrait – and portraiture in general,
which had always been a favourite subject matter.

*"I've done the portrait of Mr Gachet with an expression of melancholy,
which might often appear to be a grimace to those looking at the canvas.
And yet that's what should be painted, because then one can realise,
compared to the calm ancient portraits, how much expression there is in our
present-day heads, and passion and something like waiting and a shout.
Sad but gentle but clear and intelligent, that's how many portraits should
be done, that would still have a certain effect on people at times."*

Vincent intended to create expression, whether in a portrait or a
landscape. Over the years he had also given expression to some
of the buildings he painted. The village church in Auvers was a
substantial piece of architecture with a long nave, tall bell-tower
and apsidal chapels. Vincent confronted its east end to compress its
volume into a characterful shape. His love of linear detail is shown
in the attention he gave the late Gothic tracery of the windows. The
several sloping roofs, the buttresses and the decoration of the tower

are all detailed in paler tones than the rest of the walls. A deep blue sky serves as a backdrop to the church – the colour is repeated to soften the mass of bleak stone.

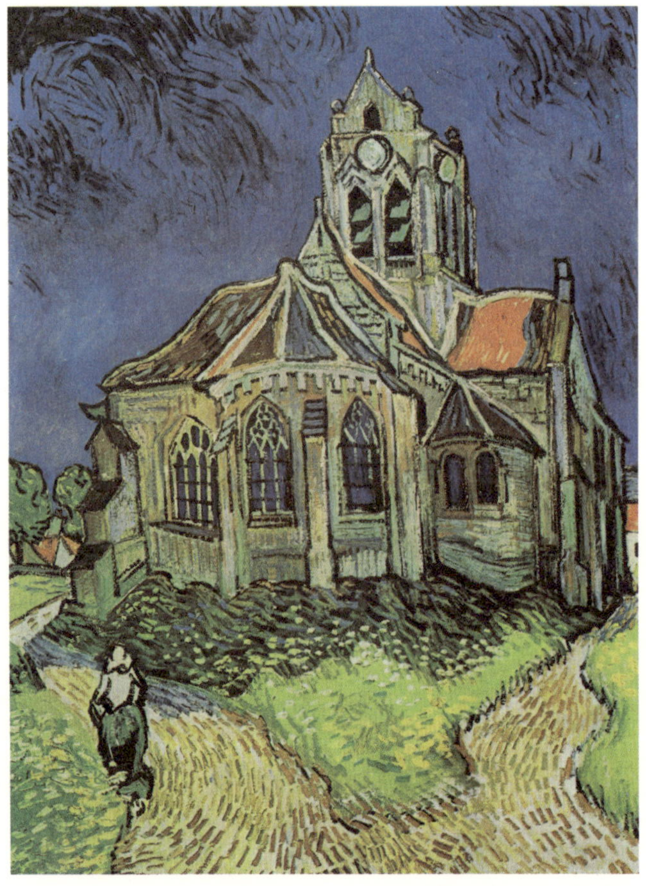

The Church at Auvers, 1890

Vincent's use of colour in this portrait of a building reveals his continuing awareness of complementaries. A reddish tone is introduced on one roof and in the background houses. The patch of green is dotted with yellow and white. The diverging paths, where a single figure walks, contain a mirror image of the church's shape.

"It's again almost the same thing as the studies I did in Nuenen of the old tower and the cemetery. Only now the colour is probably more expressive."

As Theo gave his brother news from Paris, the state of his own health was of growing concern. With uncertainty at work, he was again thinking of leaving Goupil's to branch out on his own. The risk this involved, now he had a family, needed careful thought. He wrote to Vincent for comfort.

'Look old fellow, do everything for your health, I too will do as much, we have too much in our heads for us to forget the daisies and the freshly stirred clods of earth, and the branches of the bushes that bud in spring, nor the bare tree branches that shiver in the winter, nor the serene skies of limpid blue, nor the big clouds of autumn, nor the uniformly grey sky in winter, nor the sun as it rose above our aunt's garden, nor the red sun setting in the sea at Scheveningen, nor the moon and the stars one fine night in summer or winter, no, whatever happens, that is our possession.'

Theo claimed memories of the past could act as healing compensation for difficult times in the present. Although he lived in the city, he reminded his brother of their profound love of nature that was born in their childhood. Theo's consoling words, however, would not be enough to remove Vincent's lifelong feelings of exile from home.

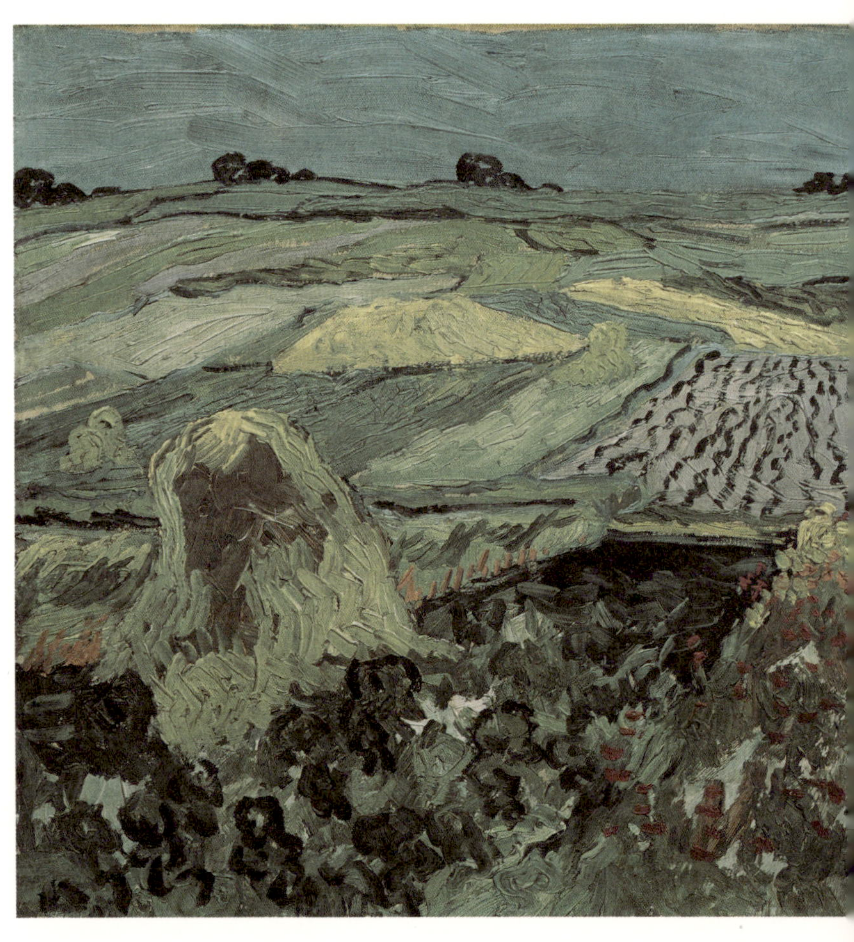

Wheatfields near Auvers, 1890

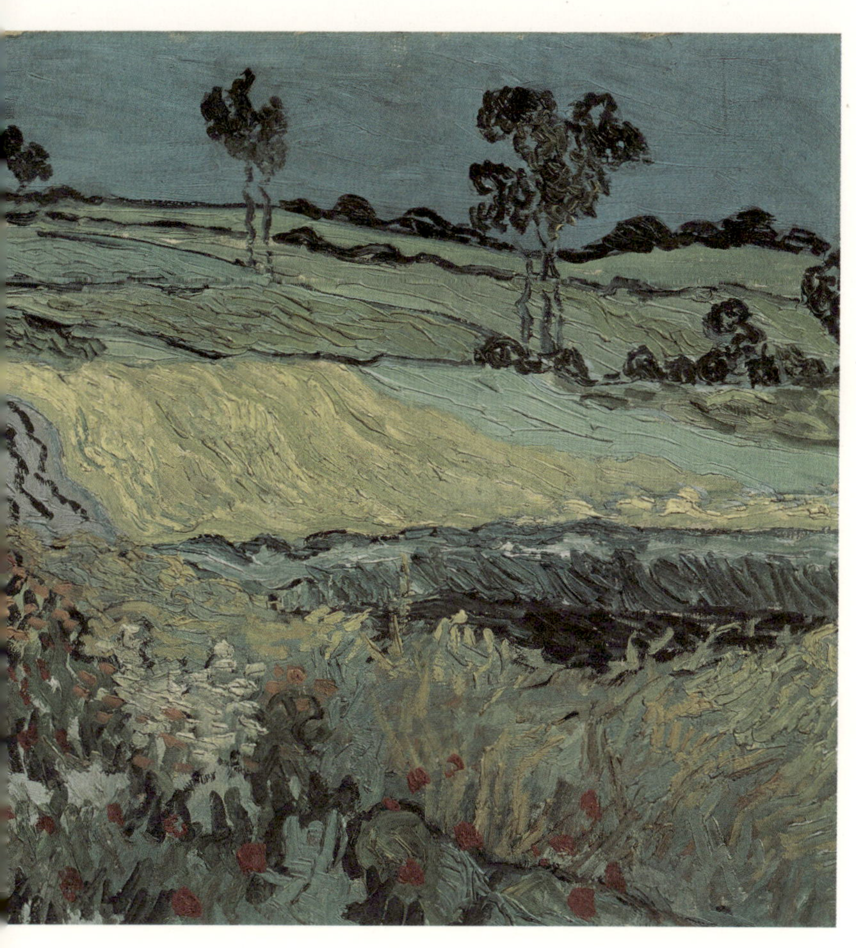

Up on the plateau above the village, Vincent watched the summer's progress and the ripening of wheat, now in less bright sunlight than he had seen in the south. His preference for wide views was well accommodated in the use of double-size canvases. He stood with a far-reaching view of fields ahead of him and showed their crops of varying textures. He compared his painting to the work of a Barbizon painter, Georges Michel (1763–1843).

Vincent still revered many artists who had come before him. Although he had gained several good reviews of his own work, he was recognised only by his avant-garde contemporaries. Gauguin, who now was thinking of going to the tropics, again wrote to tell Vincent of their appreciation of his work: 'Despite your ailing state you have never worked with so much balance while conserving the sensation and the interior warmth needed for a work of art, precisely in an era when art is a business regulated in advance by cold calculations.'

Vincent's hope that Theo and his family would come to Auvers had not left his mind. They visited one Sunday and were received at Dr Gachet's home. Later, when the baby became ill, Theo considered a return to Holland rather than Auvers. Anxiety was mounting. Theo's own illness was not helped by his firm's negative reaction to his demand for a rise in salary.

Early in July, Vincent visited them in Paris. It was a memorably bad occasion. Theo and Jo were exhausted with worry and the apartment became the scene of unexpected disruption. Vincent was unhappy with the way his paintings were stored there. A discussion over whether to move to a larger apartment – rather than the country – also arose. Jo's brother Andries contributed to the idea of starting up an independent gallery again. Visitors arrived to see Vincent, including Aurier who had written the long article, praising his work. Toulouse-Lautrec, always good company, made them laugh at lunch, but tempers flew. Vincent soon left to return to Auvers. Later Lautrec recalled the occasion.

'Vincent recalled the rather difficult and laborious hours for us all that I shared with you. It's no small thing when all together we feel the daily bread in danger, no small thing when for other causes than that we also feel our existence to be fragile.'

In the summer Auvers was filled with visitors from the city and further afield. Many people were attracted to its pleasant location near the river and open countryside. After two months there, Vincent was beginning to be a familiar sight to the inhabitants of the village. He was also unlike them. If they made fun of his unique appearance, as people in Arles had done, he found a way of hiding any offence this caused him. Doggedly, he carried on working. He returned to the wheatfields above Auvers, which he painted under turbulent skies. Through these he said he was trying to express sadness and extreme loneliness.

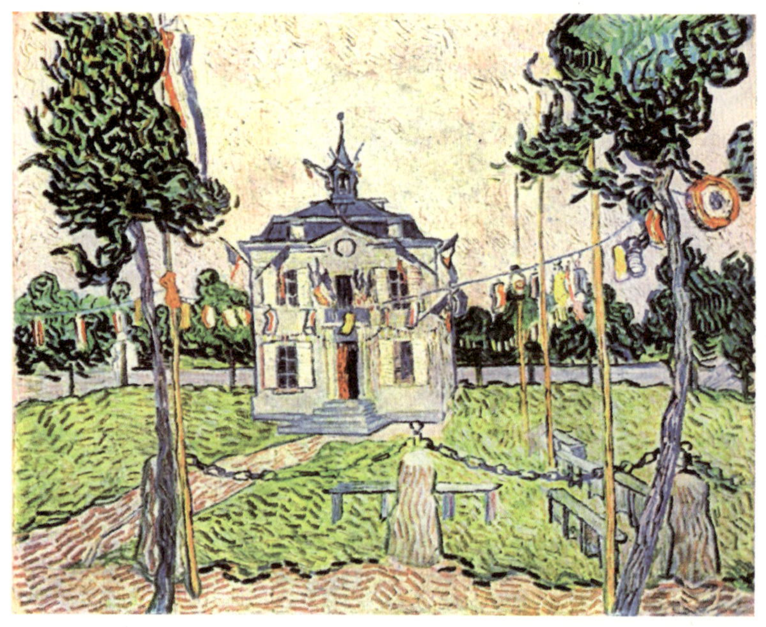

The Town Hall at Auvers, 1890

For 14 July, the town hall of Auvers was decked with festive ribbons, flags and all the paraphernalia that went with celebrating French National Day. The square where it stood was only footsteps away from Vincent's auberge. Here, centre-stage, the building becomes another portrait in Vincent's hands. Yellow cobblestones, wavering green branches and the tricolour French flag all contribute to his chosen colour scheme. But there are no people – no holidaymakers, no locals, no teasing youths, no lovers. Vincent placed the cube-like structure in the middle of the empty square. Its pale façade with windows round an open, red-tinged door replaces any human face.

When Jo visited her family in Holland, Theo described the emptiness
he felt in their apartment without her and the baby. He joined her
briefly and met up with his own family members, and described to
Vincent how pleased they all were with their new relative. On his
return to Paris, Theo faced the continuation of his job where money
fell short of his needs. As well as his wife and child, and his own ill
health, Theo had Vincent's future to consider. He told Jo his thoughts
about his brother's present state of mind and mentioned the paintings
he was working on.

'If only he could find someone to buy a couple from him, but I'm afraid
this could still take a very long time. But one cannot drop him when
he's working so hard and so well. When will a happy time come for
him? He's so thoroughly good and helped me so much to keep going.'

One day Vincent left the auberge and walked away armed with his
painting equipment. Hours later he returned with a fatal gunshot
wound beneath his ribs that took his life two days later. Theo was
with him when he died.

In his last known letter to Theo, Vincent included a sketch of the
garden of Daubigny, the painter from Barbizon who had lived in
Auvers. He was very pleased with the two painted versions he
had done and at the end of the letter he added a postscript
describing the work.

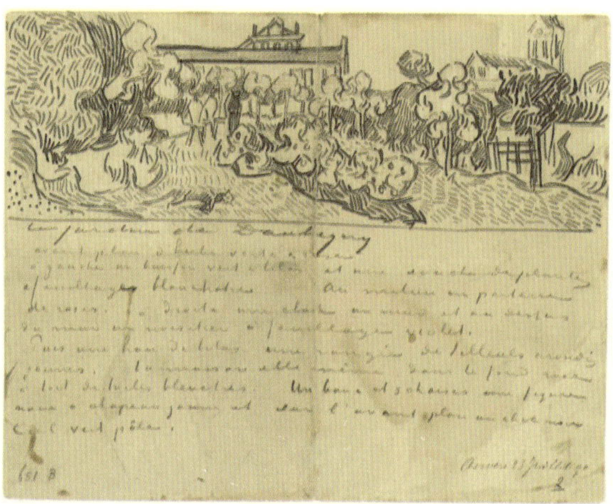

Letter to Theo van Gogh (with letter sketches of Daubigny's garden, etc.)

*"Foreground of green and pink grass, on the left a green and lilac bush and a
stem of plants with whitish foliage. In the middle a bed of roses. To the right
a hurdle, a wall, and above the wall a hazel tree with violet foliage. Then
a hedge of lilac, a row of rounded yellow lime trees. The house itself in the
background, pink with roof of bluish tiles. A bench and three chairs, a dark
figure with a yellow hat, and in the foreground a black cat. Sky pale green."*

Vincent's last words on paper were filled with brilliant colours,
as were so many of his paintings.

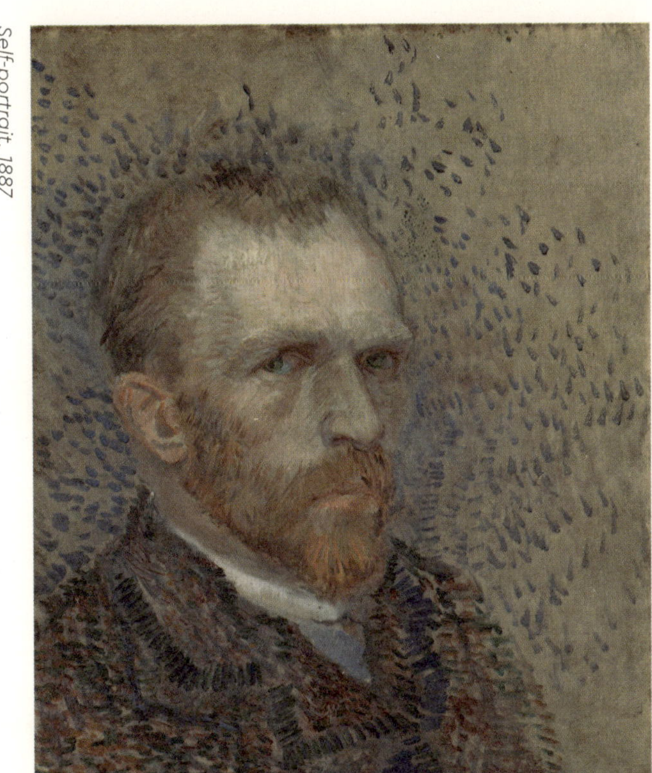

ACKNOWLEDGEMENTS:

All quotations from Van Gogh's letters have been taken
from the website **vangoghletters.org**

p.108 Kröller Müller Museum, courtesy of Wikimedia Commons; p.110 Van Gogh Museum, Amsterdam (Vincent van Gogh Foundation); p.112 Private Collection, courtesy of Wikimedia Commons; p.114 Kröller Müller Museum, courtesy of Wikimedia Commons; p.115 Hermitage Museum, courtesy of Wikimedia Commons; p.116 Rijksmuseum, courtesy of Wikimedia Commons; p.118 Kupferstichkabinett, courtesy of Wikimedia Commons; p.119 Kupferstichkabinett, courtesy of Wikimedia Commons; p.121 Museum of Fine Arts, courtesy of Wikimedia Commons; p.123 Yale University Art Gallery; p.125 Van Gogh Museum, courtesy of Wikimedia Commons; p.126 Musée d'Orsay, courtesy of Wikimedia Commons; p.129 Pushkin Museum of Fine Arts, courtesy of Wikimedia Commons; p.130 Private Collection, courtesy of Wikimedia Commons; p.132 Hermitage Museum, courtesy of Wikimedia Commons; p.135 Heritage Image Partnership Ltd / Alamy Stock Photo; p.137 Private Collection, courtesy of Wikimedia Commons; p.139 Sammlung Oskar Reinhart, courtesy of Wikimedia Commons; p.140 Private Collection, courtesy of Wikimedia Commons; p.141 Kröller Müller Museum, courtesy of Wikimedia Commons; p.143 Ny Carlsberg Glyptotek, courtesy of Wikimedia Commons; p.144 National Gallery, courtesy of Wikimedia Commons; p.147 Van Gogh Museum, courtesy of Wikimedia Commons; p.149 Indianapolis Museum of Art, courtesy of Wikimedia Commons; p.153 Van Gogh Museum, courtesy of Wikimedia Commons; p.155 Van Gogh Museum, courtesy of Wikimedia Commons; p.157 Kröller Müller Museum, courtesy of Wikimedia Commons; p.159 courtesy of Wikimedia Commons; p.160 Musee d'Orsay, courtesy of Wikimedia Commons; p.161 Private Collection, courtesy of Wikimedia Commons; p.164 Musée d'Orsay, courtesy of Wikimedia Commons; p.166–7 Österreichische Galerie Belvedere, courtesy of Wikimedia Commons; p.170 courtesy of Wikimedia Commons; p.172 Van Gogh Museum, Amsterdam (Vincent van Gogh Foundation); p.173 Van Gogh Museum, courtesy of Wikimedia Commons;